SharePoint Solutions
A Practical User Guide

Kiet Huynh

Table of Contents

Introduction

1.1 What is SharePoint?

SharePoint is a powerful web-based platform developed by Microsoft that enables organizations to create, manage, and share content and information. It serves as a comprehensive solution for document management, collaboration, and business process automation, making it an indispensable tool for organizations of all sizes.

In this section, we'll explore the key aspects of SharePoint, including its purpose, history, core features, and how it fits into modern work environments.

The Purpose of SharePoint

At its core, SharePoint is designed to streamline information sharing and collaboration within teams, departments, and entire organizations. It provides a centralized space where employees can:

- **Store and Manage Documents**: SharePoint enables users to organize and secure files in libraries, ensuring that critical documents are easy to find and share.

- **Collaborate Seamlessly**: Teams can work on projects together, with features like real-time co-authoring and discussion boards fostering communication and teamwork.

- **Automate Business Processes**: With tools like workflows and Power Automate integration, SharePoint simplifies repetitive tasks, enhancing productivity.

- **Create Custom Solutions**: Organizations can build intranet sites, dashboards, and applications tailored to their specific needs.

By addressing these key functions, SharePoint helps businesses reduce inefficiencies and enhance their overall operations.

A Brief History of SharePoint

SharePoint has evolved significantly since its initial release in 2001. Here's a snapshot of its journey:

1. **2001**: SharePoint Portal Server 2001 marked Microsoft's first attempt at a web-based collaboration tool. Its primary focus was on document management and enterprise search.

2. **2003**: Windows SharePoint Services 2.0 introduced team sites, making it easier for groups to collaborate and share information.

3. **2007**: SharePoint 2007 was a milestone, integrating new features like workflows, Excel Services, and better content management.

4. **2010 and 2013**: These versions added social networking capabilities, enhanced search, and integration with cloud services.

5. **2016**: SharePoint moved further into the cloud with SharePoint Online, part of the Microsoft 365 suite.

6. **Today**: SharePoint Online and SharePoint Server coexist, offering flexibility for cloud-based and on-premises solutions. The platform now incorporates advanced AI, mobile capabilities, and deeper integration with Microsoft Teams and Power Platform.

Core Features of SharePoint

SharePoint offers a robust set of features that cater to a wide range of business needs. Let's dive into its most prominent functionalities:

1. **Sites and Workspaces**

   o SharePoint allows organizations to create intranet sites for internal communication, project management, and more.

   o Team sites provide a dedicated space for groups to collaborate on specific tasks or projects.

   o Communication sites are perfect for sharing news and updates across the company.

2. **Document Libraries**

   o SharePoint's document libraries enable structured file storage with version control, metadata tagging, and powerful search capabilities.

   o Users can collaborate on files simultaneously with co-authoring features.

3. **Lists and Databases**

   o SharePoint lists help users manage structured data, such as task lists, issue trackers, and calendars.

   o Custom views and filters allow for better data visualization and management.

4. **Integration with Microsoft 365**

   o SharePoint integrates seamlessly with Microsoft 365 apps like Word, Excel, PowerPoint, and Teams.

   o Users can access SharePoint files directly from other applications, streamlining workflows.

5. **Automation and Workflows**

   o SharePoint supports automating repetitive tasks with Power Automate, formerly known as Microsoft Flow.

   o Built-in workflows help with approvals, notifications, and other business processes.

6. **Search and Insights**

   o Advanced search features allow users to find documents, sites, and people quickly.

   o Integration with Power BI enables organizations to create data-driven dashboards and reports.

7. **Security and Permissions**

   o SharePoint provides robust security controls, including user permissions, data encryption, and compliance with regulatory standards.

    o   Administrators can control who has access to what content, ensuring data confidentiality.

How SharePoint Fits into Modern Work Environments

In today's increasingly remote and digital work environment, SharePoint plays a critical role in bridging gaps between team members.

1. **Facilitating Remote Work**

   o   With SharePoint Online, employees can access documents and collaborate from anywhere in the world.

   o   Mobile applications for iOS and Android extend SharePoint's functionality to smartphones and tablets.

2. **Centralizing Knowledge and Information**

   o   SharePoint serves as a single source of truth for organizational knowledge.

   o   Features like news feeds, wikis, and document libraries ensure that everyone is aligned and informed.

3. **Supporting Hybrid Work Models**

   o   SharePoint integrates with Microsoft Teams, making it easier for hybrid teams to collaborate.

   o   Offline capabilities in SharePoint enable work continuity even in low-connectivity scenarios.

Benefits of Using SharePoint

Organizations that leverage SharePoint often experience numerous advantages, including:

1. **Improved Collaboration**

   o   SharePoint breaks down silos by fostering better communication and collaboration across teams.

2. **Enhanced Productivity**

    o By automating routine tasks and centralizing resources, SharePoint enables employees to focus on high-value work.

3. **Cost Efficiency**

    o As part of Microsoft 365, SharePoint eliminates the need for multiple standalone tools, reducing overall IT costs.

4. **Scalability**

    o SharePoint can grow with an organization, accommodating everything from small teams to enterprise-level operations.

5. **Customizability**

    o Organizations can tailor SharePoint sites and solutions to meet specific business needs without extensive coding.

Conclusion

SharePoint is more than just a tool; it's a platform that transforms how businesses operate. From managing documents to fostering collaboration and automating processes, SharePoint's capabilities are vast and versatile.

Understanding what SharePoint is and how it functions lays the foundation for utilizing its features effectively. The next sections of this guide will delve deeper into how you can maximize SharePoint to meet your organizational goals.

1.2 Why Use SharePoint?

SharePoint has become one of the most popular and widely adopted tools for businesses and organizations around the globe. Its versatility and robust features empower teams to collaborate effectively, streamline workflows, and enhance productivity. In this section, we'll delve into the key reasons why organizations choose SharePoint as their go-to solution for managing information, fostering collaboration, and driving efficiency.

Centralized Collaboration Platform

One of the main advantages of SharePoint is its ability to centralize collaboration. In traditional workflows, team members often struggle with disconnected tools, redundant tasks, and fragmented communication. SharePoint addresses these challenges by offering a unified platform where teams can share files, discuss projects, and coordinate tasks seamlessly.

- **Real-Time Collaboration:** SharePoint supports simultaneous editing, allowing multiple users to work on the same document at the same time. This feature eliminates version conflicts and ensures that everyone is on the same page.

- **Document Sharing and Access Control:** With its advanced permissions system, you can easily control who has access to specific documents or folders, enhancing security without hampering collaboration.

For organizations managing large teams, SharePoint's ability to integrate with Microsoft Teams further elevates its value, enabling even richer collaboration experiences.

Streamlined Document Management

Managing documents effectively is a critical need for most businesses. SharePoint excels in this area, offering features such as version control, metadata tagging, and automated workflows.

- **Version History:** SharePoint automatically tracks changes made to documents, enabling users to revert to earlier versions if necessary. This is particularly useful in legal, academic, or creative fields where document integrity is crucial.

- **Metadata Tagging:** Users can categorize documents with custom metadata tags, making it easier to search and filter through extensive libraries.

- **Automated Approval Workflows:** SharePoint automates routine tasks, such as document approvals, reducing manual effort and improving efficiency.

Organizations with regulatory compliance requirements also benefit from SharePoint's document retention policies and audit trails.

Enhanced Communication and Engagement

In large organizations, maintaining effective communication can be challenging. SharePoint provides tools to foster engagement, ensuring that teams stay informed and connected.

- **Intranet Portals:** SharePoint allows companies to create branded intranet sites that serve as a central hub for announcements, policies, and updates.

- **News Posts:** Teams can quickly publish news articles or updates, ensuring that all employees are aware of critical developments.

- **Discussion Boards:** These enable teams to hold threaded discussions, ask questions, and share ideas in a structured manner.

SharePoint's ability to integrate with Yammer further enhances internal communication, allowing for more informal and dynamic exchanges.

Integration with Microsoft Ecosystem

SharePoint seamlessly integrates with the broader Microsoft 365 suite, including tools like Outlook, Word, Excel, Teams, and Power BI. This integration enables users to perform tasks without switching between platforms, saving time and reducing errors.

- **Outlook Integration:** Attach SharePoint documents directly to emails or link files instead of sending large attachments.

- **Power BI Dashboards:** Embed live data visualizations into SharePoint pages to provide teams with actionable insights.

- **Teams Channels:** Link SharePoint libraries to Microsoft Teams, ensuring that all project-related files are easily accessible within team channels.

This level of integration positions SharePoint as a powerful productivity enhancer for businesses already using Microsoft tools.

Scalability and Flexibility

SharePoint's scalability makes it suitable for organizations of all sizes, from small startups to multinational corporations. Its flexible architecture allows businesses to tailor their SharePoint environment to their unique needs.

- **Custom Solutions:** Developers can create custom apps, workflows, and integrations using tools like Power Automate and Power Apps.

- **Industry-Specific Use Cases:** Whether it's a healthcare provider managing patient records or a construction company tracking project timelines, SharePoint's adaptability ensures relevance across industries.

- **Multi-Language Support:** SharePoint supports multiple languages, enabling global teams to collaborate effectively.

The ability to scale resources as an organization grows ensures that SharePoint remains a viable long-term solution.

Security and Compliance

In today's digital landscape, data security is paramount. SharePoint offers robust security features to protect sensitive information while ensuring compliance with industry regulations.

- **Role-Based Permissions:** Granular access controls prevent unauthorized access to files and folders.

- **Data Encryption:** SharePoint encrypts data both at rest and in transit, safeguarding it against breaches.

- **Compliance Features:** Organizations in regulated industries can benefit from SharePoint's built-in compliance tools, such as eDiscovery and legal holds.

These features make SharePoint an attractive option for businesses that prioritize security without compromising functionality.

Mobile Accessibility

As remote work and on-the-go access become increasingly common, SharePoint ensures users can stay connected regardless of their location.

- **Mobile App:** The SharePoint mobile app allows users to access sites, files, and news on their smartphones or tablets.

- **Responsive Design:** SharePoint's web interface is optimized for mobile devices, ensuring a seamless experience.

- **Offline Access:** Users can sync files to their devices for offline use, making SharePoint a practical choice for teams working in remote or low-connectivity areas.

Cost Efficiency

By consolidating multiple tools and workflows into a single platform, SharePoint reduces the need for additional software, leading to significant cost savings.

- **Cloud Hosting:** With SharePoint Online, businesses save on infrastructure costs associated with on-premises solutions.

- **Subscription Plans:** SharePoint's flexible pricing options cater to organizations with varying budgets.

For businesses looking to maximize ROI, SharePoint's robust feature set justifies its cost.

Conclusion

SharePoint's diverse capabilities make it an indispensable tool for modern organizations. Whether it's streamlining document management, fostering team collaboration, enhancing communication, or ensuring data security, SharePoint delivers immense value across various business functions. By adopting SharePoint, organizations can not only improve their operational efficiency but also empower their teams to achieve greater success.

This chapter has explored the key reasons why SharePoint stands out as a leading solution. In the next section, we'll take a closer look at the different types of SharePoint solutions and how to choose the one that best fits your organization's needs.

1.3 Overview of SharePoint Solutions

Microsoft SharePoint is a dynamic platform that combines a variety of tools and functionalities to improve collaboration, enhance productivity, and streamline workflows within organizations. Whether you're managing documents, building an intranet, or automating workflows, SharePoint offers tailored solutions to address diverse business needs. In this section, we'll explore key SharePoint solutions and how they can be applied effectively in real-world scenarios.

Centralized Document Management

One of SharePoint's most celebrated features is its ability to centralize document management. Organizations often struggle with scattered files stored across different locations, creating inefficiencies and security risks. SharePoint resolves this by providing a centralized repository where files can be stored, accessed, and managed securely.

Key Benefits:

- **Version Control**: Automatically tracks changes made to documents, allowing users to access previous versions when needed.

- **Co-Authoring**: Enables multiple users to work on a document simultaneously, enhancing team collaboration.

- **Permission Settings**: Ensures sensitive information is only accessible to authorized personnel.

Use Case Example:

A multinational company uses SharePoint to manage its policy documents. Employees across offices access the most up-to-date files from a centralized location, reducing errors caused by outdated information.

Team Collaboration Sites

SharePoint team sites act as digital hubs where teams can collaborate efficiently. Each team site is equipped with tools for file sharing, task management, and communication, fostering an environment of transparency and productivity.

Features of a Team Site:

- **Document Libraries**: Share and store files related to specific projects.

- **Task Lists**: Track and assign tasks with clear deadlines and priorities.

- **Calendars**: Synchronize team schedules and events.

Use Case Example:

A marketing team creates a SharePoint site to coordinate a product launch. They store campaign assets, assign tasks to team members, and schedule meetings, all within the site, eliminating reliance on multiple tools.

Communication Sites

While team sites focus on internal collaboration, communication sites are designed for broader audiences. These sites are perfect for sharing news, reports, or other information with the entire organization or specific departments.

Highlights of Communication Sites:

- **Visually Engaging Layouts**: Templates that support rich media content such as images, videos, and news posts.

- **Audience Targeting**: Ensures relevant content is displayed to specific groups.

- **Customizable Web Parts**: Add features like weather updates, countdown timers, or external links.

Use Case Example:

An HR department uses a communication site to share company announcements, employee handbooks, and training schedules with the entire workforce.

Workflow Automation

SharePoint, integrated with Microsoft Power Automate, empowers users to automate repetitive tasks, saving time and reducing human errors. Workflows can range from simple approval processes to complex multi-step operations.

Popular Automated Workflows:

- **Document Approval**: Automatically route files to supervisors for review and approval.

- **Employee Onboarding**: Create automated checklists and reminders for onboarding new hires.

- **Expense Reporting**: Simplify the process of submitting and approving expense claims.

Use Case Example:

A finance team automates their invoice approval process. When a new invoice is uploaded to a SharePoint library, the system notifies the relevant manager, who can approve or reject it directly via email.

Intranet and Corporate Portals

SharePoint is widely used to build corporate intranets, acting as a central hub for organizational communication, resources, and collaboration. These portals can be customized to reflect a company's branding and meet specific business needs.

Key Features of Intranets:

- **News Feeds**: Keep employees updated with the latest announcements.

- **Resource Libraries**: Provide access to company policies, templates, and training materials.

- **Employee Directories**: Make it easy to find contact information for coworkers.

Use Case Example:

A technology firm creates an intranet on SharePoint where employees can find everything from IT support resources to cafeteria menus, improving accessibility and engagement.

Data Integration and Analytics

SharePoint's ability to integrate with tools like Power BI allows organizations to turn raw data into actionable insights. Users can create interactive dashboards and reports that are accessible directly from SharePoint.

Integration Capabilities:

- **Power BI Dashboards**: Embed real-time analytics to monitor performance metrics.

- **Excel Integration**: Connect and share Excel-based data for reporting.

- **Third-Party Tools**: Link SharePoint with CRMs, ERPs, or other business tools.

Use Case Example:

A sales department integrates SharePoint with their CRM system to generate live sales performance dashboards, enabling the team to make data-driven decisions.

Content and Knowledge Management

SharePoint excels in organizing and managing large volumes of content. Using metadata and tagging, users can locate information quickly, ensuring that valuable knowledge is not lost in clutter.

Features Supporting Content Management:

- **Metadata Tags**: Categorize files for easier search and retrieval.

- **Search Optimization**: Leverage SharePoint's powerful search capabilities to find specific documents or information.

- **Knowledge Bases**: Create repositories for FAQs, tutorials, and best practices.

Use Case Example:

A consulting firm builds a knowledge base on SharePoint, compiling case studies, templates, and best practices for employees to reference during projects.

External Sharing and Collaboration

SharePoint makes it easy to collaborate with external stakeholders, such as clients or vendors, while maintaining strict security protocols.

Features for External Collaboration:

- **Guest Access**: Allow external users to access specific files or sites.

- **Sharing Links**: Set expiration dates and permissions for shared links.

- **Secure Workspaces**: Create dedicated spaces for external collaboration.

Use Case Example:

An event management company collaborates with vendors by sharing project timelines and resources via a secure SharePoint site.

Conclusion

SharePoint is a versatile platform offering a range of solutions tailored to diverse organizational needs. From document management to data analytics and intranet building, SharePoint helps businesses streamline operations, foster collaboration, and achieve efficiency. By understanding these solutions, users can unlock the full potential of SharePoint and drive meaningful impact in their workplace.

1.4 How to Use This Guide

This guide is designed to be your trusted companion as you navigate SharePoint's extensive ecosystem. Whether you're completely new to the platform or have some prior experience, this book provides practical insights and hands-on tips to maximize SharePoint's potential in your daily work. To help you make the most of this guide, let's outline how to approach the chapters, leverage the tools provided, and adapt the knowledge to your unique needs.

Start with Your Experience Level

SharePoint can be daunting at first, given its vast array of features and configurations. That's why this guide is structured to cater to readers of varying experience levels:

- **Beginners**: If you're new to SharePoint, focus on the early chapters, which introduce the platform's fundamentals. Learn how to set up an account, navigate the interface, and create basic sites. Pay special attention to terms like "permissions," "libraries," and "workflows," as these concepts will form the foundation for more advanced topics later.

- **Intermediate Users**: If you've already used SharePoint, start with chapters on customizing sites and managing documents. These sections will help you optimize your workflow by introducing tools like Power Automate, version control, and metadata.

- **Advanced Users**: For seasoned users looking to deepen their expertise, explore sections on integrations with Power BI, external sharing, and advanced workflow automation.

Key Features of This Guide

1. **Modular Structure**: Each chapter builds on the previous one but is also self-contained. You can jump directly to topics of interest without needing to follow a strict order.

2. **Detailed Walkthroughs**: Practical, step-by-step instructions accompany every key feature of SharePoint. For example, you'll learn how to create a document library, set permissions, or embed a Power BI dashboard directly into your site.

3. **Real-World Examples**: Throughout the guide, you'll find case studies and examples of how organizations use SharePoint effectively. These illustrate best practices and common pitfalls to avoid.

4. **Visual Aids**: Screenshots, diagrams, and tables make complex processes easier to follow. Whenever a topic involves multiple steps, we've provided annotated visuals to guide you.

How to Apply the Knowledge

SharePoint is highly customizable, and its functionality often depends on how your organization has configured it. Here's how you can adapt this guide to your environment:

- **Follow Along with Practice**: Whenever possible, work through the exercises in real-time. For instance, if you're reading about creating a team site, try replicating the steps in your own SharePoint account.

- **Consult with IT or Admins**: If certain features aren't available in your SharePoint instance, reach out to your IT team. Some functionalities may require admin permissions or additional licensing.

- **Experiment Safely**: Use a sandbox or test environment if your organization provides one. This allows you to explore features without risking disruptions to live sites or data.

Making the Most of Chapters

- **Introduction**: Gain a foundational understanding of what SharePoint is and why it's a critical tool for modern collaboration. If you're unsure how SharePoint fits into your workflow, this section will clarify its potential benefits.

- **Creating and Managing Sites**: Learn the building blocks of SharePoint. Whether you need a team site for project collaboration or a communication site for sharing updates, this chapter walks you through setup and customization.

- **Document Management**: Arguably the most used feature of SharePoint, document libraries are essential for storing, sharing, and collaborating on files. This chapter will teach you about version control, metadata, and best practices for organization.

- **Advanced Features**: SharePoint's integrations with tools like Power BI and Teams make it a powerhouse for productivity. Use these sections to unlock advanced functionality that can transform how your team works.

Tips for Successful Learning

1. **Set Goals**: Determine what you want to achieve with SharePoint. Are you looking to streamline document management, improve team collaboration, or create an intranet? Let these goals guide your learning path.

2. **Take Notes**: As you progress, jot down key steps or tips. SharePoint's interface may change slightly over time, so having personal notes can help you adapt.

3. **Leverage Additional Resources**: While this guide is comprehensive, SharePoint is a vast platform. Use Microsoft's official documentation, community forums, and YouTube tutorials to supplement your learning.

4. **Practice Consistently**: SharePoint is best learned through hands-on experience. Dedicate time to exploring its features and applying them to real-world scenarios.

FAQs for Using This Guide

- **Do I need prior technical knowledge to use this book?** No! This guide assumes no prior experience with SharePoint or other Microsoft tools. However, familiarity with basic IT concepts like file sharing and permissions will be helpful.

- **What version of SharePoint does this guide cover?** This guide focuses on SharePoint Online, the cloud-based version integrated with Microsoft 365. Many features are also applicable to on-premises versions, but specific configurations may differ.

- **What if I encounter a problem not covered in the book?** SharePoint's community forums and Microsoft's support pages are excellent resources. Additionally, consulting your organization's IT team can often resolve issues unique to your setup.

Staying Up-to-Date with SharePoint

Microsoft frequently updates SharePoint, adding new features and refining existing ones. As you use this guide, keep an eye on the latest updates by subscribing to Microsoft's SharePoint blog or newsletter.

By following the structure and advice laid out in this chapter, you'll be equipped to make the most of this book and SharePoint itself. Dive into the next section to begin your journey with confidence, and let's unlock the potential of SharePoint together!

Page 24 | 274

CHAPTER I
Getting Started with SharePoint

1.1 Setting Up Your SharePoint Account

1.1.1 Creating an Account

Setting up a SharePoint account is the first step to harnessing its capabilities for collaboration and productivity. Whether you are part of a large organization, a small team, or an individual looking to streamline your work, creating an account ensures that you have access to the features and tools SharePoint offers. This section will guide you through the process, explain the prerequisites, and provide helpful tips to avoid common pitfalls.

Understanding the Basics of a SharePoint Account

A SharePoint account is typically linked to a Microsoft 365 subscription. Organizations often manage SharePoint accounts centrally through IT administrators, but individuals and small teams can also create accounts independently by purchasing the necessary subscription. Here are the essentials:

- **Microsoft 365 Subscription**: SharePoint is a component of Microsoft 365, so a valid subscription is required. The subscription type (e.g., Business, Enterprise, or Personal) will dictate the features and limits available to your account.

- **Email Address Requirement**: An active email address is necessary to register and verify your account. For organizational accounts, this is often your work email.

- **Administrator Access (For Organizations)**: If you're setting up an account for a team or company, ensure you have administrator rights to configure settings and permissions.

Step-by-Step Guide to Creating a SharePoint Account

Step 1: Accessing the Microsoft 365 Portal

To begin, navigate to the Microsoft 365 website at https://www.microsoft.com/microsoft-365. If your organization has already set up Microsoft 365, you might have a direct SharePoint link through your corporate intranet. For individual or small team accounts, you will need to sign up for Microsoft 365 first.

- Click on the **Sign Up** or **Get Started** button.

- Choose a subscription plan that suits your needs. If you're uncertain, Microsoft provides a comparison of plans, highlighting features like storage capacity, user limits, and included applications.

Step 2: Register Your Account

- **Personal Information**: Enter your full name, email address, and contact details.

- **Payment Information**: If this is a paid plan, provide your payment details to activate the subscription. Free trials are available for new users who wish to explore the platform before committing.

- **Verification**: Confirm your email address through a verification link sent to your inbox. For organizational accounts, your IT department may handle this step.

Step 3: Setting Up Your SharePoint Environment

After successfully creating your Microsoft 365 account, you'll be redirected to the admin dashboard. Here, you can activate and configure SharePoint:

1. Log in to the Microsoft 365 admin center using your new credentials.

2. Navigate to the **Apps** section and locate SharePoint.

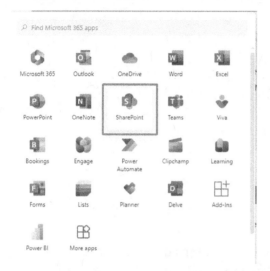

3. Click on **Activate** or **Launch** to initialize your SharePoint environment.

Configuring Your SharePoint Account

Once your account is active, it's essential to configure it to meet your specific needs. SharePoint's flexibility allows you to tailor the experience, whether you are using it for document management, team collaboration, or as an intranet platform.

Profile Settings

- Update your profile with accurate details, such as your job title, profile picture, and contact information. This helps colleagues identify you within the SharePoint ecosystem.

- Ensure your time zone and regional settings are correctly configured to avoid scheduling issues and date formatting errors.

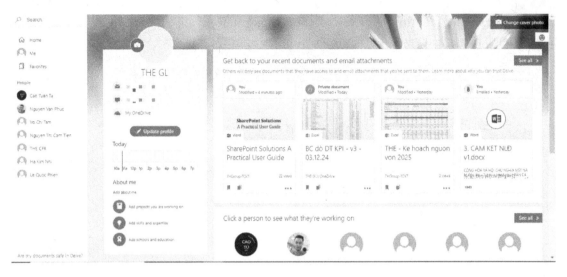

Security Settings

- Choose a strong password that complies with Microsoft's security recommendations.

- Enable multi-factor authentication (MFA) for added security. This step is crucial for protecting sensitive data stored in SharePoint.

Choosing Your Default Language

SharePoint supports multiple languages. Select the language that best suits your team or organization. This setting can be updated later if needed.

Common Challenges and Troubleshooting

Despite its user-friendly interface, some users may encounter challenges when setting up a SharePoint account. Below are common issues and solutions:

- **Issue: Email Verification Not Received**

  o **Solution**: Check your spam or junk folder. If the problem persists, ensure the email address was entered correctly during registration.

- **Issue: Payment Declined**

  o **Solution**: Verify the payment method details and ensure your account has sufficient funds. Contact Microsoft support if the issue remains unresolved.

- **Issue: Access Denied for Team Members**
  - o **Solution**: Confirm that permissions are assigned correctly in the admin center. Users may need to be added manually to the SharePoint group.

Benefits of a Well-Set-Up Account

Creating your SharePoint account is more than a technical step—it lays the foundation for seamless collaboration and efficient workflows. With an account properly set up, you gain access to:

- **Document Sharing and Collaboration**: Store, share, and edit files with team members in real time.

- **Enhanced Team Communication**: Centralize discussions and updates through SharePoint's integrated tools.

- **Streamlined Project Management**: Use SharePoint to track tasks, deadlines, and progress.

Conclusion

The process of creating a SharePoint account may seem straightforward, but attention to detail can make a significant difference in your overall experience. By following the steps outlined above, you'll ensure that your account is set up efficiently and securely. This sets the stage for exploring the powerful features SharePoint has to offer, which we'll dive into in the next sections of this guide.

1.1.2 Accessing SharePoint Online

Accessing SharePoint Online is a fundamental step in starting your SharePoint journey. Whether you're a beginner or transitioning from on-premises versions, this section will guide you through everything you need to know to access SharePoint Online seamlessly. From understanding the prerequisites to navigating the platform, you'll gain a comprehensive overview that ensures you're ready to collaborate effectively.

Understanding the Requirements for Access

Before accessing SharePoint Online, ensure you meet the following prerequisites:

1. **Microsoft 365 Subscription**: SharePoint Online is a cloud-based service that is part of the Microsoft 365 suite. You'll need a valid subscription to Microsoft 365 that includes SharePoint.

2. **Internet Connection**: A stable and reliable internet connection is essential for accessing SharePoint Online since it operates entirely through the web.

3. **Browser Compatibility**: Use a compatible web browser for the best experience. SharePoint Online works seamlessly with modern browsers such as Microsoft Edge, Google Chrome, Safari, and Mozilla Firefox.

Logging into SharePoint Online

Follow these steps to access SharePoint Online:

1. **Open Your Web Browser**: Launch your preferred web browser on your computer or mobile device.

2. **Navigate to the Microsoft 365 Portal**: Enter the URL https://www.office.com into your browser's address bar. This will take you to the Microsoft 365 login page.

3. **Sign In with Your Credentials**: Enter your Microsoft 365 email address and password. If your organization uses multi-factor authentication (MFA), you'll need to complete the verification process using a phone, email, or app-based code.

4. **Locate the SharePoint App**: Once logged in, you'll see a dashboard featuring various Microsoft 365 apps. Click on the SharePoint icon to open SharePoint Online.

5. **Select Your SharePoint Site**: Depending on your organization's setup, you might see a list of frequently accessed or featured sites. Select the site you need to access, or use the search bar to locate it.

Accessing SharePoint Through the Mobile App

Microsoft offers a SharePoint mobile app for iOS and Android devices, making it easy to stay connected on the go. Here's how to get started:

1. **Download the App**: Visit the App Store or Google Play Store and search for "Microsoft SharePoint." Download and install the app.

2. **Sign In to Your Account**: Open the app and log in using your Microsoft 365 credentials.

3. **Navigate to Your Sites**: The app will display a list of sites you frequently visit. You can also use the search function to find specific content.

4. **Sync Files for Offline Access**: Enable offline access to important files by syncing them directly to your device.

Navigating the SharePoint Online Environment

Once logged into SharePoint Online, you'll find several key components that form the backbone of your collaboration:

1. **Homepage**: The SharePoint homepage offers a centralized view of your frequently accessed sites, recent activity, and news posts.

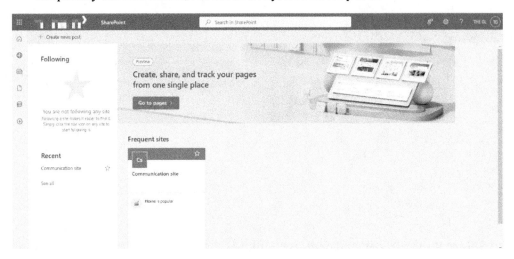

2. **Site Collections**: These are individual sites within your organization's SharePoint ecosystem. Each site is designed for specific projects, teams, or departments.

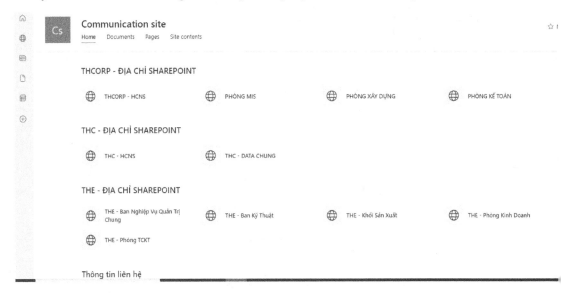

3. **Quick Launch Menu**: This menu appears on the left side of the screen and provides quick access to libraries, lists, and other resources within a site.

4. **Search Functionality**: SharePoint's powerful search tool allows you to locate files, documents, or sites quickly. Simply type a keyword or phrase into the search bar.

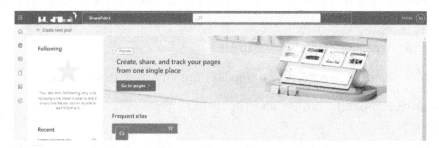

5. **Settings and Help**: The gear icon in the top-right corner provides access to settings and help documentation for customizing your SharePoint experience.

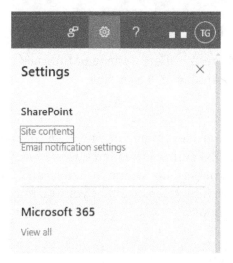

Troubleshooting Access Issues

If you encounter challenges while trying to access SharePoint Online, consider these common scenarios and solutions:

1. **Forgotten Credentials**: Use the "Forgot Password" link on the Microsoft 365 login page to reset your password. Contact your organization's IT department if needed.

2. **Browser Compatibility Issues**: Clear your browser cache or try accessing SharePoint from a different browser.

3. **Account Permissions**: Ensure that your account has the appropriate permissions to access specific sites. If not, reach out to your SharePoint administrator.

4. **Multi-Factor Authentication (MFA) Problems**: Double-check your verification method and ensure your device is set up correctly for MFA.

Best Practices for Accessing SharePoint Online

To maximize your SharePoint experience, consider the following best practices:

1. **Bookmark Important Links**: Save the URLs of frequently accessed sites for quick navigation.

2. **Enable Notifications**: Stay informed about updates and changes by enabling notifications for critical sites and documents.

3. **Keep Credentials Secure**: Avoid sharing your Microsoft 365 credentials with others, and update your password regularly.

4. **Explore Tutorials and Resources**: Microsoft offers a range of tutorials and help documentation to enhance your understanding of SharePoint.

Summary

Accessing SharePoint Online is the first step toward leveraging its powerful collaboration and document management tools. By following the steps outlined in this section, you'll be equipped to navigate the platform with ease, troubleshoot common issues, and optimize your workflow. SharePoint's flexibility and accessibility ensure that your team can work together effectively, whether in the office or remotely.

1.2 Navigating the SharePoint Interface

1.2.1 The SharePoint Homepage

The SharePoint homepage serves as the central hub for all your activities within the platform. It's designed to provide a streamlined interface that helps users access important tools, view recent activity, and manage collaboration efforts effectively. In this section, we'll break down the essential elements of the SharePoint homepage and explore how to make the most of this workspace.

Overview of the Homepage Layout

When you first log in to SharePoint, you'll land on the homepage. The layout typically includes the following sections:

1. **Top Navigation Bar**

   o Located at the very top of the page, the navigation bar provides quick links to key areas such as your organization's home site, Microsoft 365 apps, notifications, and your profile.

   o The **Search Bar**, prominently positioned, is an essential tool for finding documents, sites, or people across your SharePoint environment.

2. **Main Content Area**

   o This is the focal point of the homepage, showcasing personalized content based on your activity and permissions. It often includes:

      ▪ **Recommended Documents:** Files you recently accessed or that are relevant to your work.

      ▪ **Highlighted News Posts:** Updates and announcements shared across your organization.

      ▪ **Frequent Sites:** A list of sites you visit most often.

3. **Quick Links Section**

   o Found on the left or right-hand side, this section allows easy access to important sites, libraries, or files. Administrators can configure these links for shared access.

4. **Activity Feed**

   o This area displays recent activity across your connected sites, such as file uploads, edits, or updates.

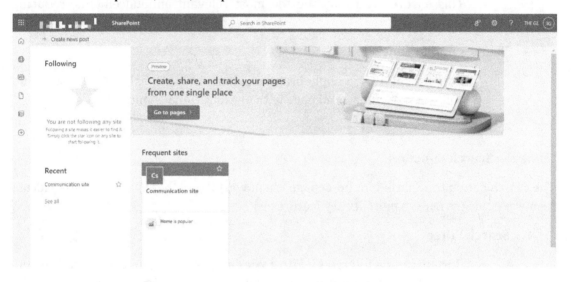

Customizing Your Homepage

One of the strengths of SharePoint is its customizability. Depending on your role and permissions, you can personalize your homepage to make it more relevant to your tasks.

1. **Pinning Important Sites**

   o Use the **Pin to Quick Access** option to prioritize frequently used sites or libraries.

   o Pinned sites appear in a designated section, saving you time navigating through menus.

2. **Organizing Quick Links**

- o Customize the Quick Links section by adding, rearranging, or removing items.

- o To add a link, click the **Edit** button, select **Add a Link**, and provide the URL and title.

3. **Adjusting News Feed Preferences**

- o Tailor the news feed to display updates from specific sites or projects.

- o This ensures you only see the most relevant announcements, reducing clutter.

4. **Themes and Layouts**

- o Administrators can apply branding elements, such as company logos and colors, to align the homepage with organizational standards.

Using the Search Function

The search bar on the SharePoint homepage is a powerful tool that enables users to locate resources quickly. Let's explore its key features:

1. **Search Filters**

- o Results can be filtered by **File Type** (e.g., Word documents, Excel sheets), **Author**, or **Date Modified**, allowing for more precise searches.

- o Advanced search options let you search within specific sites or libraries.

2. **Intelligent Suggestions**

- o As you type, SharePoint's intelligent search predicts what you're looking for, offering suggestions based on your activity history.

3. **People and Groups Search**

- o Use the search bar to find colleagues or groups, making it easy to connect or collaborate.

Navigating Between Sites

The homepage acts as a gateway to all your SharePoint sites. Understanding how to navigate efficiently can enhance your productivity:

1. **Site Directory**

   o Click on the **Sites** tab in the top navigation bar to view a directory of all the sites you have access to.

   o Use the search bar or filters to locate specific sites.

2. **Hub Sites**

   o If your organization uses hub sites, these will appear prominently on your homepage.

   o Hub sites aggregate content from related sites, providing a unified view of projects or departments.

3. **Frequent Sites and Followed Sites**

   o The homepage dynamically displays sites you frequently visit or choose to follow, allowing for quick access.

Best Practices for Navigating the Homepage

1. **Bookmark Key Resources**

   o Save links to essential sites or files for easy access during busy workdays.

2. **Leverage Personalized Recommendations**

   o Pay attention to the recommended content section to stay updated on relevant documents and activities.

3. **Stay Organized with Quick Links**

   o Regularly review and update your Quick Links to ensure they remain relevant to your current projects.

4. **Engage with News Posts**

   o Use the like, comment, and share features to interact with news posts, fostering collaboration and communication within your organization.

Common Challenges and How to Overcome Them

1. **Overwhelming Content**

   o If the homepage feels cluttered, customize the layout to focus on the tools and sections you use most.

2. **Difficulty Finding Resources**

   o Make full use of the search bar and filters to locate documents or sites quickly.

3. **Inconsistent Updates**

   o Ensure that the homepage is updated regularly, especially the news feed and Quick Links section, to reflect current priorities.

By mastering the SharePoint homepage, users can significantly enhance their workflow efficiency, collaboration capabilities, and overall experience. Understanding its layout and features is a crucial first step in navigating SharePoint confidently.

1.2.2 Key Features and Tools

Navigating SharePoint's interface is essential for maximizing productivity and collaboration. SharePoint offers a wide range of features and tools designed to support efficient document management, seamless communication, and robust team coordination. This section will explore the primary tools and features you'll encounter in the SharePoint interface, breaking them down into categories for ease of understanding and application.

1. Navigation Bar

The navigation bar, often found at the top of the SharePoint interface, serves as a central hub for accessing various parts of your SharePoint environment.

1. **Home Button**: Provides quick access to the SharePoint homepage, where users can see an overview of their sites, tasks, and notifications.

2. **Search Bar**: This tool allows users to locate documents, people, or sites quickly. SharePoint's search functionality is enhanced with AI to provide suggestions as you type, making it easier to find the right resources.

3. **App Launcher**: The waffle icon in the navigation bar connects SharePoint with other Microsoft 365 apps like Teams, OneDrive, and Outlook, ensuring seamless integration.

2. SharePoint Sites

SharePoint sites are the foundation of the platform. They come in different types, each tailored to specific collaboration needs.

1. **Team Sites**: Designed for group collaboration, these sites offer shared workspaces for files, lists, and communication. Commonly used by project teams or departments.

2. **Communication Sites**: These sites focus on broadcasting information across an organization. They feature visually engaging layouts ideal for company news or announcements.

3. **Hub Sites**: Hub sites unify related SharePoint sites, providing a central location for shared navigation, news rollups, and activity feeds.

3. Document Libraries

One of SharePoint's core functionalities is document storage and management. Document libraries are specialized repositories where users can upload, share, and manage files.

1. **Version History**: SharePoint automatically tracks changes to documents, allowing users to view or revert to previous versions if needed.

2. **Check-In/Check-Out**: This feature ensures that multiple users do not overwrite each other's changes. Users can "check out" a document for editing and "check it in" once done.

3. **Metadata**: SharePoint allows users to tag documents with metadata for easier categorization and searchability. For example, you can assign tags like "Invoice" or "Proposal" to files.

4. Lists

Lists in SharePoint provide a structured way to organize and track information. Think of them as customizable tables where you can store data for various purposes.

1. **Custom Lists**: Users can create lists from scratch, adding columns to capture specific types of information.

2. **Templates**: SharePoint offers pre-built list templates for tasks, contacts, and issue tracking, saving time and effort.

3. **Integration with Microsoft Power Automate**: Lists can be connected to workflows, automating repetitive tasks like sending reminders or updating status fields.

5. Pages and Web Parts

SharePoint pages are customizable canvases where users can display content. These pages often include **web parts**, which are modular components that add functionality to a page.

1. **News Web Part**: Displays recent news posts, helping teams stay informed about updates.

2. **Document Library Web Part**: Embeds a document library directly on a page for easy access.

3. **Calendar Web Part**: Displays upcoming events, deadlines, or meetings.

4. **Custom Web Parts**: Users with advanced permissions can develop custom web parts to meet specific needs.

6. Search and Discoverability

The SharePoint search engine is a powerful tool designed to save time and increase productivity.

1. **Search Refiners**: After performing a search, users can narrow results by criteria like file type, date modified, or author.

2. **Delve Integration**: Delve provides personalized content recommendations based on user activity and connections, making it easier to discover relevant information.

3. **Saved Searches**: Frequent searches can be saved for quick future access, especially useful for recurring tasks.

7. Permissions Management

Permissions determine who can access or modify content within SharePoint. The platform allows fine-grained control over access rights.

1. **Role-Based Permissions**: Assign roles like "Owner," "Member," or "Visitor" to control access levels.

2. **Sharing Settings**: Easily share documents or folders with internal or external users. You can set expiration dates or passwords for added security.

3. **Audit Logs**: Administrators can track user actions, such as file downloads or permission changes, for transparency and accountability.

8. Integration with Microsoft 365

SharePoint seamlessly integrates with other Microsoft 365 tools, enabling a connected workflow.

1. **Teams Integration**: SharePoint libraries can be added to Microsoft Teams channels for instant access.

2. **OneDrive**: Personal file storage in OneDrive can sync with SharePoint libraries, allowing users to access files offline.

3. **Outlook**: SharePoint calendars and task lists can sync with Outlook for better scheduling and time management.

9. Communication Tools

SharePoint supports internal communication through various features designed to enhance collaboration.

1. **Announcements**: Team sites can display announcements for team members to see important updates.

2. **News Posts**: Communication sites can broadcast updates organization-wide, complete with visuals and formatting.

3. **Alerts**: Users can set alerts for changes to documents or libraries, ensuring they stay informed of updates.

10. Mobile Compatibility

SharePoint's mobile app ensures users can stay connected, even on the go.

1. **Mobile-Friendly Interface**: Sites automatically adjust to fit mobile screens, making navigation seamless.

2. **Push Notifications**: The app sends alerts for site activity, ensuring you never miss an update.

3. **Offline Access**: Documents and lists can be accessed offline, with changes syncing once reconnected.

Conclusion

Mastering the key features and tools in SharePoint is crucial for maximizing its potential as a collaboration platform. Whether it's using document libraries to manage files or leveraging lists for tracking data, these features empower teams to work smarter and more efficiently. By becoming familiar with the tools outlined in this section, you'll be well-equipped to navigate SharePoint with confidence and make the most of its robust capabilities.

1.3 Understanding Permissions and Access

1.3.1 User Roles Explained

Permissions in SharePoint form the backbone of collaboration and content security. To effectively manage access, it is crucial to understand the concept of user roles and how they influence what actions users can perform within a SharePoint site. This section explores the fundamental roles in SharePoint, their capabilities, and how they align with organizational needs.

The Importance of Roles in SharePoint

User roles define the scope of activities individuals can perform on a SharePoint site. These roles help ensure that users have access to the right information while maintaining security. Assigning roles appropriately avoids unauthorized changes, safeguards sensitive data, and enhances team efficiency by aligning permissions with specific responsibilities.

Key benefits of defining roles effectively include:

- **Controlled Access:** Restricts users to view or edit only the necessary content.

- **Security Compliance:** Helps meet data security and privacy standards.

- **Collaboration Enhancement:** Ensures users can work together without interference.

Default SharePoint Roles

SharePoint provides a set of default roles, known as **permission levels**, designed to meet common collaboration and management needs. Each role includes a predefined set of permissions tailored for specific tasks:

1. **Owner**

    o The **Owner** role grants full control over the site.

    o Owners can manage site settings, add or remove users, and adjust permissions for all other roles.

o   Typically assigned to site administrators or project managers responsible for maintaining the site.

Common Actions by Owners:

o   Customizing the site structure and appearance.

o   Configuring security settings and permissions.

o   Overseeing content organization and workflows.

2. **Member**

o   Members have permissions to contribute content, such as uploading documents, adding list items, and editing shared materials.

o   Ideal for team members actively working on projects hosted within the site.

Common Actions by Members:

o   Creating and editing documents.

o   Commenting on shared materials.

o   Participating in discussions or updating project tasks.

3. **Visitor**

o   Visitors have **read-only access**, allowing them to view content without making any modifications.

o   Suitable for stakeholders who need oversight but do not contribute directly.

Common Actions by Visitors:

o   Viewing reports, announcements, or project updates.

o   Accessing shared links or read-only dashboards.

4. **Custom Roles**

o   Organizations can create custom roles to address unique requirements not covered by the default options.

o For example, a "Reviewer" role might allow commenting without editing rights.

Creating Custom Roles:

o Identify specific tasks and permissions required for the role.

o Use the **Advanced Permissions Settings** in SharePoint to configure granular permissions.

Understanding Permission Inheritance

Permission inheritance is a core feature of SharePoint that simplifies managing access across sites and subsites. By default, subsites inherit permissions from their parent site. This ensures consistency but can be customized for unique access needs.

Advantages of Permission Inheritance:

- Streamlines permission management by reducing redundant configurations.

- Ensures that changes to parent site permissions propagate to all subsites.

Breaking Inheritance:

- In some scenarios, subsites or libraries may require unique permissions.

- Administrators can "break inheritance" to customize permissions for specific users or groups.

Best Practices for Assigning Roles

To maximize efficiency and security, consider these best practices when assigning roles:

1. **Adopt the Principle of Least Privilege**

    o Grant users only the permissions they need to perform their tasks.

    o Avoid assigning roles like Owner to users who don't require administrative privileges.

2. **Use Groups to Manage Permissions**

    o Instead of assigning roles to individual users, create **groups** in SharePoint.

- o For example, a "Marketing Team" group can have Member access, while "Executives" may have Visitor access.

- o This approach simplifies permissions management when team members join or leave.

3. **Audit Permissions Regularly**

- o Periodically review site permissions to ensure they align with current project needs.

- o Remove access for users who no longer require it to enhance security.

4. **Document Permission Changes**

- o Maintain a log of role assignments and permission changes.

- o This documentation is especially valuable for auditing and compliance purposes.

Examples of Real-World Role Assignments

Scenario 1: Project Collaboration Site

- **Owner:** Project Manager

- **Member:** Team members actively contributing to tasks and deliverables.

- **Visitor:** Stakeholders who need periodic updates but don't participate in daily work.

Scenario 2: Company-Wide Communication Site

- **Owner:** IT Administrator

- **Member:** Department heads who post announcements or manage pages.

- **Visitor:** All employees who need access to read company updates.

Troubleshooting Common Role Issues

Issue 1: Unauthorized Access Errors

- Cause: Users may be assigned insufficient permissions for specific actions.

- Solution: Verify the assigned role and upgrade permissions if necessary.

Issue 2: Overlapping Permissions

- Cause: Users might belong to multiple groups with conflicting roles.

- Solution: Check group memberships and resolve permission conflicts.

Issue 3: Inadvertent Permission Changes

- Cause: Owners or Members may accidentally modify access levels.

- Solution: Use SharePoint's **Audit Logs** to identify and reverse unintended changes.

Summary

Understanding user roles in SharePoint is essential for efficient site management and secure collaboration. The built-in roles of Owner, Member, and Visitor provide a solid foundation, while custom roles and permission inheritance allow for tailored access control. By following best practices and actively managing roles, administrators can foster a productive and secure SharePoint environment.

1.3.2 Managing Permissions

Managing permissions is one of the core responsibilities when working with SharePoint. Permissions determine who can access, view, edit, and manage content within a SharePoint site. Understanding how to assign and control permissions ensures the security and efficient collaboration of your team. This section will guide you through the fundamentals of managing permissions effectively.

What Are Permissions in SharePoint?

Permissions in SharePoint dictate the level of access a user or group has to specific content, such as sites, libraries, lists, or individual files. These permissions are typically structured into **permission levels**, which include predefined roles like:

- **Full Control:** Grants complete control over the site, including settings and permissions.

- **Edit:** Allows users to view, add, update, and delete content.

- **Contribute:** Enables users to add and modify content but restricts site settings.

- **Read:** Provides view-only access to the content.

Understanding these levels helps administrators assign the right permissions based on the role and responsibility of each user or group.

Assigning Permissions to Users and Groups

Assigning permissions in SharePoint involves providing access to individual users or groups. Here's a step-by-step guide:

1. **Access the Site Permissions Settings:**

   o Navigate to the site where you want to manage permissions.

   o Click on the **Settings Gear** icon in the top-right corner.

   o Select **Site Permissions** from the dropdown menu.

2. **Add Users or Groups:**

   o In the **Site Permissions** panel, click **Grant Permissions**.

   o Enter the email addresses of users or select a predefined group.

   o Choose the appropriate permission level (e.g., Read, Edit, or Full Control).

   o Add a message (optional) to notify the user about their access.

   o Click **Share** to finalize the changes.

3. **Use Groups for Efficient Permission Management:**

   SharePoint allows the creation of **groups**, which act as containers for permissions. Instead of assigning permissions to individual users, you can assign them to a group and add users to that group. This approach simplifies managing access, especially for larger teams. Common default groups include:

   o **Owners:** Full Control access.

- o **Members:** Edit access.
- o **Visitors:** Read-only access.

Understanding Permission Inheritance

SharePoint uses a concept called **permission inheritance**, where child elements (like lists or libraries) inherit permissions from their parent site. This inheritance can be broken if specific elements require unique access control.

How to Break Permission Inheritance:

1. Navigate to the item (e.g., document library, list, or page) you want to modify.
2. Open the settings for that item.
3. Select **Advanced Permissions Settings**.
4. Click **Stop Inheriting Permissions** from the ribbon.
5. Adjust permissions as needed for the specific item.

When to Break Inheritance:

Breaking inheritance is useful when:

- A document requires restricted access (e.g., sensitive reports).
- Specific team members need exclusive edit rights to a list or library.
- Compliance requirements mandate segregated access to certain content.

Best Practices for Managing Permissions

Proper permission management ensures a secure and productive SharePoint environment. Consider these best practices:

1. **Follow the Principle of Least Privilege:**
   - o Assign users the minimum permissions necessary to perform their tasks.
   - o Avoid granting Full Control unless absolutely required.

2. **Use Groups Instead of Individuals:**
   - Manage permissions at the group level to simplify administration.
   - Keep group membership updated to reflect team changes.

3. **Regularly Audit Permissions:**
   - Periodically review who has access to your sites and content.
   - Remove access for users who no longer need it.

4. **Document Permission Changes:**
   - Maintain a record of who has access and what permissions were granted.
   - Note any custom permissions applied to specific items.

5. **Educate Users on Permissions:**
   - Provide basic training on how permissions work.
   - Encourage users to report if they encounter access issues.

Troubleshooting Permissions Issues

Even with careful planning, permissions issues can arise. Below are some common problems and solutions:

1. **User Cannot Access Content:**
   - Verify that the user is assigned the appropriate permissions.
   - Check if the item inherits permissions from the parent site.

2. **User Has More Access Than Expected:**
   - Inspect all groups the user belongs to and their associated permission levels.
   - Check for broken inheritance or unique permissions applied to the item.

3. **Shared Links Not Working:**

- o Ensure the link settings align with the intended level of access (e.g., view-only vs. edit).

- o Verify the sharing settings for the site or library.

Using Advanced Permission Features

SharePoint offers advanced tools to streamline permission management:

1. **SharePoint Admin Center:**

   For site collection administrators, the SharePoint Admin Center provides a centralized interface to manage permissions across multiple sites.

2. **Auditing and Reporting:**

   - o Use audit logs to track permission changes and identify potential security issues.

   - o Generate reports to review who has access to sensitive content.

3. **Power Automate for Access Requests:**

   Automate the approval process for access requests using Power Automate, reducing administrative overhead and ensuring proper oversight.

Conclusion

Effectively managing permissions in SharePoint is critical for maintaining security and promoting collaboration. By understanding permission levels, leveraging groups, and applying best practices, you can ensure that your SharePoint environment operates smoothly and securely. Whether you're assigning access to a new team member or troubleshooting an issue, mastering permission management will empower you to maximize the potential of SharePoint as a collaborative tool.

CHAPTER II
Creating and Managing Sites

2.1 Types of SharePoint Sites

2.1.1 Team Sites vs. Communication Sites

In the SharePoint ecosystem, understanding the distinction between **Team Sites** and **Communication Sites** is crucial for setting up the right kind of environment to meet your organizational needs. While both types of sites offer unique features and advantages, their purposes, audiences, and capabilities differ significantly. This section explores these two core types of SharePoint sites, guiding you on when and how to use each effectively.

What Are Team Sites?

Team Sites are designed to foster collaboration among a specific group of people. These sites are typically used for internal projects, departmental initiatives, or group activities where teamwork, document sharing, and task management are central.

Key Features of Team Sites

1. **Document Libraries**

   Team Sites include shared document libraries where team members can upload, store, and collaborate on files in real time. Version control ensures that all edits are tracked, making it easy to revert to previous versions if needed.

2. **Shared Calendars**

   With integrated calendars, teams can schedule meetings, track project milestones, and manage deadlines efficiently.

3. **Task Lists and Planner Integration**

Team Sites provide built-in task management tools, such as task lists or integration with Microsoft Planner, to help assign responsibilities and monitor progress.

4. **Permissions Management**
   Team Sites allow for role-based permissions, so only authorized users have access to specific content. For instance, team members can have edit access while stakeholders may only have view permissions.

5. **Integration with Microsoft Teams**

   Many organizations use Team Sites alongside Microsoft Teams. Files shared in Teams channels are automatically stored in a linked SharePoint Team Site, creating a seamless collaboration experience.

When to Use Team Sites

- When your focus is on **collaborative work**.

- For managing **project-based teams** or **departmental initiatives**.

- When frequent file sharing, co-authoring, and ongoing communication are required.

- For small to medium-sized groups where every member actively contributes to the site content.

What Are Communication Sites?

Communication Sites, on the other hand, are tailored for broadcasting information to a larger audience. These sites are often used to share news, updates, policies, or any other information intended for consumption rather than collaboration.

Key Features of Communication Sites

1. **Modern Page Design**

   Communication Sites emphasize visual storytelling. They include customizable modern pages with web parts for images, text, and videos to create visually engaging layouts.

2. **News Publishing**

These sites excel in publishing news articles or announcements to a broad audience, making them ideal for corporate communications.

3. **Audience Targeting**

With audience targeting, you can personalize content so that specific groups see information relevant to them, enhancing the user experience.

4. **Mobile-Friendly Interface**

Communication Sites are optimized for mobile devices, ensuring content looks great and remains accessible on any screen size.

5. **Search-Driven Content**

Built-in search capabilities help users quickly find information, such as company policies, HR guidelines, or training resources.

When to Use Communication Sites

- When your primary goal is **information dissemination** rather than collaboration.

- For **company-wide announcements**, such as new policies, strategic updates, or event promotions.

- When the audience is **larger and more diverse**, such as all employees across departments.

- For **external-facing content**, like partner or customer portals.

Key Differences: Team Sites vs. Communication Sites

Feature	Team Sites	Communication Sites
Purpose	Collaboration and teamwork	Sharing information broadly
Audience	Specific groups or teams	Large, diverse audiences
Design	Functional and task-focused	Visual and content-focused
Permissions	Role-based, tightly managed	Often open for broader visibility
Use Cases	Project management, file sharing	Corporate announcements, updates

Choosing the Right Site for Your Needs

When deciding between a Team Site and a Communication Site, consider the following:

1. **Collaboration vs. Communication**

   If your goal is to encourage collaboration among a group of users who need to share files, work on documents simultaneously, and track project tasks, a **Team Site** is the way to go. For example, a marketing team collaborating on a campaign would benefit from a Team Site.

On the other hand, if the goal is to share information with a wide audience, such as an announcement about a new company policy, a **Communication Site** is more appropriate.

2. **Audience Size and Role**

   A **smaller, engaged group** works best with a Team Site where everyone contributes actively. A **larger audience** that primarily consumes information fits better with a Communication Site.

3. **Visual Requirements**

   For visually appealing layouts with a focus on design and aesthetics, opt for a Communication Site. Team Sites, while customizable, are more utility-driven and less visually focused.

Hybrid Scenarios: Using Both Site Types Together

There are scenarios where combining Team Sites and Communication Sites can maximize productivity. For instance:

- A project team uses a **Team Site** to manage their daily tasks and files.

- Simultaneously, they use a **Communication Site** to share project updates, milestones, and results with company executives or other departments.

This dual-site approach leverages the strengths of each type, ensuring efficient teamwork while maintaining effective communication.

By understanding the differences between **Team Sites** and **Communication Sites**, you can create a SharePoint environment that aligns with your organization's needs, enhances collaboration, and ensures clear communication. Both types of sites serve distinct purposes, and choosing the right one—or a combination of both—can significantly improve workflow efficiency and user satisfaction.

2.1.2 Hub Sites Explained

Hub sites are one of the most powerful features in SharePoint, designed to bring together related sites and create a unified structure for content and collaboration. In this section, we'll dive into what hub sites are, how they function, and why they're essential for a well-organized SharePoint environment. Whether you're managing a single department or an entire organization, hub sites can streamline navigation, improve communication, and ensure consistency across your SharePoint sites.

What is a Hub Site?

A hub site in SharePoint acts as a central hub for connecting and organizing multiple related SharePoint sites. Think of it as the spine of your organization's intranet, linking team sites, communication sites, or other SharePoint sites into a cohesive system.

Key features of hub sites include:

- **Centralized Navigation:** Hub sites offer a shared navigation bar that appears across all associated sites, making it easier for users to find information quickly.

- **Unified Branding:** By linking sites to a hub, you can apply consistent branding, themes, and layouts, ensuring a cohesive look and feel.

- **Aggregated Content:** Hub sites consolidate news, events, and activities from associated sites into one place, helping teams stay informed.

- **Search Across Sites:** When users perform a search on a hub site, they can see results from all the connected sites, making information retrieval more efficient.

When to Use Hub Sites

Hub sites are particularly useful in the following scenarios:

1. **Departmental Organization:** Large organizations often have multiple departments, each with their own team sites. A hub site can link these sites

together under a single department hub, enabling employees to access all related resources easily.

2. **Project Portfolios:** For companies that manage several projects simultaneously, hub sites can connect individual project sites, providing an overview of project updates, resources, and progress.

3. **Regional Management:** Global organizations with offices in different regions can use hub sites to organize regional sites, while still maintaining a unified corporate structure.

4. **Knowledge Management:** A hub site can serve as a repository for knowledge-sharing, linking research, resources, and training sites under a single umbrella.

How to Create a Hub Site

Creating a hub site is a straightforward process but requires administrative permissions. Here's a step-by-step guide:

1. **Select the Site to Become the Hub:**

   Decide which site will act as the hub. This could be an existing communication site or team site, depending on your needs.

2. **Register the Site as a Hub:**

   o   Navigate to the **SharePoint Admin Center**.

- o Under **Sites**, select **Active Sites**.

- o Click on the site you want to register, then choose **Hub Site Settings**.

- o Click **Register as Hub Site**, and provide a name for the hub.

3. **Associate Sites to the Hub:**

- o Open the settings of a site you want to associate with the hub.

- o Select **Hub Site Association** and choose the hub site from the dropdown menu.

- o Repeat this process for all related sites.

Active sites

Use this page to sort and filter sites and change site settings.
Learn more about managing sites

+ Create   🖉 Edit   👥 Membership   🔗 Hub ∨   👥 Sharing   🏠 Change home site

Register as hub site

Site name ∨   Teams ∨

Associate with a hub

4. **Configure Navigation and Branding:**

- o Customize the hub site navigation bar to include links to frequently accessed resources.

o   Apply a consistent theme or logo to all associated sites for uniformity.

Benefits of Hub Sites

Hub sites offer a range of benefits that enhance collaboration, streamline communication, and improve user experience:

1. **Simplified Navigation:**

   Users no longer need to remember URLs or navigate through multiple layers of unrelated sites. The shared navigation bar provides a logical structure for accessing related content.

2. **Consistent Look and Feel:**

   Applying a unified theme ensures that all sites under the hub appear consistent, reinforcing your organization's branding.

3. **Improved Content Visibility:**

   Aggregated news, announcements, and events from associated sites keep everyone informed without requiring users to visit multiple sites.

4. **Enhanced Search Capabilities:**

   Searching on a hub site surfaces results from all connected sites, reducing the time spent hunting for information.

5. **Streamlined Site Management:**

   Hub sites allow admins to manage multiple sites as a group, making it easier to implement updates, permissions, and branding changes.

Best Practices for Using Hub Sites

1. **Plan Your Hub Site Structure Carefully:**

   Before creating hub sites, map out your organization's needs. Consider the relationships between departments, projects, or regions, and design a logical structure that reflects these connections.

2. **Limit the Number of Hub Sites:**

To avoid confusion, limit the number of hub sites in your organization. Each hub should represent a distinct area of focus or organizational unit.

3. **Keep Navigation Simple:**

Use clear, descriptive labels in the hub navigation bar. Avoid cluttering the menu with too many links.

4. **Regularly Update Associated Sites:**

Ensure that the content on associated sites remains relevant and up-to-date. Stale content can detract from the effectiveness of the hub.

5. **Monitor Hub Site Usage:**

Use the analytics features in SharePoint to track how users interact with the hub site. This data can help you refine navigation and content placement.

Common Challenges and How to Overcome Them

1. **Disorganized Site Associations:**

If sites are not properly categorized before being linked to a hub, users may struggle to find relevant content. Resolve this by auditing associated sites regularly and ensuring they align with the hub's purpose.

2. **Permission Conflicts:**

Permissions for individual sites may not always align with the hub's structure. Work with site owners to standardize permissions across all associated sites.

3. **Overcomplicating Navigation:**

A hub site with too many links or nested menus can confuse users. Focus on creating a clean, intuitive navigation experience.

Hub sites are an essential feature of SharePoint, offering a flexible and scalable way to organize related sites. By leveraging hub sites effectively, organizations can improve communication, foster collaboration, and create a seamless user experience across their intranet. As you explore the capabilities of hub sites, keep the best practices and common challenges in mind to maximize their potential.

2.2 Setting Up a SharePoint Site

2.2.1 Choosing a Template

When creating a new SharePoint site, selecting the right template is one of the most critical decisions you'll make. SharePoint offers a variety of site templates, each designed for specific purposes. This section will guide you through understanding these templates, their unique features, and how to choose the one that best fits your needs.

Understanding SharePoint Site Templates

A SharePoint site template is essentially a predefined structure with specific layouts, features, and tools tailored for different use cases. Microsoft provides templates to help users quickly set up sites without starting from scratch. These templates streamline the process of creating a site and ensure that it is equipped with the necessary tools to achieve its intended purpose.

Broadly, SharePoint site templates can be divided into two categories: **Team Sites** and **Communication Sites**. In addition, there are **Hub Sites**, which function as parent sites to connect multiple related sites.

Popular Templates and Their Use Cases

Here's an overview of some common SharePoint templates and how they can be used:

1. **Team Site Template**:

   o **Purpose**: Facilitates collaboration within a team or department.

   o **Features**: Document libraries, task lists, shared calendars, and discussion boards.

   o **Use Case**: Ideal for internal projects, task management, and file sharing among team members.

2. **Communication Site Template**:

- o **Purpose**: Designed for sharing information broadly across an organization.

- o **Features**: Visual storytelling tools like image galleries, news posts, and a customizable homepage.

- o **Use Case**: Perfect for announcements, organizational updates, or sharing reports.

3. **Project Site Template**:

- o **Purpose**: Manages a specific project and tracks its progress.

- o **Features**: Task tracking tools, project timelines, and calendars.

- o **Use Case**: Suitable for temporary projects that require task delegation and reporting.

4. **Blog Site Template**:

- o **Purpose**: Enables publishing of blogs or updates within an organization.

- o **Features**: Blog posts, comment sections, and categories for posts.

- o **Use Case**: Sharing knowledge, best practices, or team announcements.

5. **Hub Site Template**:

- o **Purpose**: Connects related sites and centralizes information.

- o **Features**: Unified navigation, search functionality across associated sites, and site activity aggregation.

- o **Use Case**: Bringing together departmental or regional sites under a single umbrella.

Key Factors to Consider When Choosing a Template

To make the most of your SharePoint site, carefully evaluate your requirements and match them to the features of available templates. Below are some factors to consider:

1. Purpose of the Site

- Ask yourself: What is the primary goal of this site? If it's for team collaboration, a **Team Site** would be appropriate. If it's for broadcasting information, opt for a **Communication Site**.

2. Audience

- Determine the audience for your site. For a small, internal team, choose templates like **Team Sites** or **Project Sites**. For larger audiences, such as company-wide communications, use a **Communication Site**.

3. Required Features

- Identify the features you'll need. For example, if you need extensive file sharing and co-authoring capabilities, go with a **Team Site**. If visual storytelling is your priority, a **Communication Site** will provide the necessary tools.

4. Customization Needs

- Consider how much customization you're willing to do. Predefined templates like **Blog Sites** are highly specific, while **Team Sites** allow for greater flexibility in customization.

5. Scalability and Integration

- If your site needs to integrate with other tools or scale over time, **Hub Sites** can provide the necessary infrastructure. These templates allow you to manage multiple connected sites effectively.

Step-by-Step Guide to Choosing a Template

1. **Access the Site Creation Menu**:

    o Go to your SharePoint homepage and click the **Create Site** button.

    o You'll be presented with options to select a template.

2. **Review the Available Templates**:

o Carefully read the descriptions provided for each template. Microsoft often includes sample visuals and feature highlights.

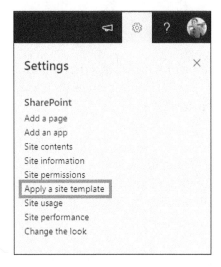

3. **Preview the Templates**:

o Most templates come with a preview option. Use this to explore the layout and features before making a final decision.

4. **Match the Template to Your Needs**:

o Refer back to the factors discussed above. Choose a template that aligns with your goals and audience.

5. **Select the Template and Customize It**:

    o Once selected, proceed to customize the site's name, description, and privacy settings.

Real-World Examples

Example 1: Marketing Department Collaboration

The marketing team at a mid-sized company needed a central location to store campaign assets, collaborate on documents, and track progress. They chose a **Team Site** template, allowing them to integrate with Microsoft Teams and maintain a shared calendar for deadlines.

Example 2: Company-Wide Announcements

A large corporation wanted a visually engaging platform for broadcasting corporate news and updates. They opted for a **Communication Site**, leveraging its image galleries and customizable layouts to create a modern, professional look.

Tips for Success

1. **Test Before Finalizing**:

    o Create a test site with your chosen template. This allows you to explore its features without impacting your actual project.

2. **Start Simple**:

    o For beginners, simpler templates like **Team Sites** are ideal. You can always add advanced features as your familiarity with SharePoint grows.

3. **Seek Feedback**:

    o If the site will be used by multiple people, involve them in the template selection process. Their input can ensure that the site meets everyone's needs.

4. **Leverage SharePoint Help Resources**:

o Microsoft provides extensive documentation and video tutorials on using SharePoint templates. Take advantage of these to make an informed decision.

By carefully selecting the right template, you'll set the foundation for a SharePoint site that is functional, user-friendly, and aligned with your organizational goals. The next step is to dive into configuring the site settings, which will be covered in **2.2.2 Configuring Site Settings**.

2.2.2 Configuring Site Settings

Configuring the settings of a SharePoint site is a crucial step to ensure it functions effectively for your team or organization. Proper configuration not only enhances usability but also ensures security, compliance, and a tailored user experience. In this section, we will explore key settings you can adjust, how to access them, and practical tips for making the most of these configurations.

Accessing Site Settings

To configure site settings in SharePoint, follow these steps:

1. **Navigate to Your Site**: Open your SharePoint site in a web browser.

2. **Access the Settings Menu**: Click the gear icon in the top-right corner of the page to open the settings menu.

3. **Choose "Site Settings"**: In the dropdown menu, select **Site Settings**. This will bring you to the configuration page where various options are available.

Key Site Settings to Configure

1. Site Name and Description

The first step in setting up your SharePoint site is to provide a clear and concise name and description.

- **Why It Matters**: A meaningful name helps users identify the purpose of the site, and a description provides context about its contents or intended use.

- **How to Configure**:

    o   Go to **Site Information** in the settings menu.

    o   Enter the desired **Site Name** and **Site Description**.

    o   Click **Save** to apply changes.

2. Privacy Settings

SharePoint offers three privacy levels for sites:

- **Private**: Only approved members can access the site.

- **Public**: Anyone in your organization can view the site.

- **Restricted Access**: Limits access to specific groups or individuals.

- **How to Configure**:

  o Navigate to **Site Permissions** from the settings menu.

  o Adjust the privacy level by selecting **Edit Privacy Settings**.

Tip: For sensitive information, always opt for **Private** and restrict permissions to essential team members only.

3. Site Permissions

Permissions determine who can view, edit, and manage the content on your site. Configuring these properly ensures that users only have access to what they need.

- **Permission Levels**:

  o **Full Control**: For site owners or administrators.

  o **Edit**: For team members who need to update content.

  o **View Only**: For users who only need to consume content.

- **How to Configure**:

  o Go to **Advanced Permission Settings** under **Site Permissions**.

  o Add or remove users or groups, and assign the appropriate permission level.

Tip: Regularly review and update permissions to ensure compliance with organizational policies.

4. Regional and Language Settings

SharePoint supports global teams by allowing you to configure regional and language preferences.

- **Key Settings**:

  o Time Zone

  o Locale

  o Default Language

- **How to Configure**:
    - Navigate to **Regional Settings** under **Site Administration**.
    - Select the appropriate options and click **Save**.

Tip: If your site is used by an international team, consider enabling multiple languages to enhance accessibility.

5. Navigation Settings

Effective navigation is critical for user experience. SharePoint allows you to customize the site's navigation bar for easy access to important content.

- **How to Configure**:
    - Go to **Navigation** under **Look and Feel**.
    - Add, remove, or reorder links.
    - Use headings to organize navigation into logical groups.

Tip: Limit the number of top-level links to avoid overwhelming users.

6. Search Settings

Configuring search settings ensures that users can quickly find the content they need.

- **Key Options**:
    - **Enable Content Search**: Make all site content searchable.
    - **Customize Search Results**: Highlight specific types of content.
- **How to Configure**:
    - Navigate to **Search Settings** under **Site Administration**.
    - Adjust the options as needed.

Advanced Configuration Options

1. Site Features

SharePoint includes optional features you can activate to enhance functionality, such as workflows, metadata navigation, and publishing tools.

- **How to Configure**:

    o   Go to **Manage Site Features** under **Site Actions**.

    o   Enable or disable features as required.

2. Site Collection Features

For administrators managing multiple sites, site collection features offer additional tools and functionalities across all sites in the collection.

- **How to Configure**:

    o   Navigate to the **Site Collection Features** section.

    o   Enable features like **Enterprise Metadata** or **Document Sets**.

Best Practices for Configuring Site Settings

1. **Plan Ahead**: Before configuring your site, have a clear understanding of your team's needs and workflows.

2. **Test Settings**: Use a test environment to explore different configurations before applying them to the live site.

3. **Document Changes**: Keep a record of the settings you adjust for future reference or troubleshooting.

4. **Train Users**: Provide training or documentation to help team members understand how the site is configured and how they can use it effectively.

Common Pitfalls to Avoid

1. **Overcomplicating Permissions**: Use group-based permissions rather than assigning them individually to avoid confusion.

2. **Neglecting Navigation**: Poor navigation design can frustrate users and reduce productivity.

3. **Ignoring Security**: Ensure privacy settings and permissions are reviewed regularly to protect sensitive information.

Summary

Configuring your SharePoint site settings is a foundational step in creating a workspace that supports collaboration, enhances productivity, and ensures compliance. By carefully tailoring these settings to meet your team's specific requirements, you can unlock the full potential of SharePoint as a versatile and efficient platform.

This comprehensive guide to configuring site settings should help you build a well-organized, secure, and user-friendly SharePoint site.

2.3 Managing Site Content

2.3.1 Adding Pages and Libraries

Managing content effectively in SharePoint is critical for creating an organized and functional site. Pages and libraries form the backbone of SharePoint content management, serving as platforms for information sharing and document storage. This section provides a detailed guide to adding and configuring pages and libraries in your SharePoint site.

What Are Pages in SharePoint?

Pages in SharePoint are customizable spaces where you can display content, embed web parts, and organize information for your users. They serve as the visual and informational interface of your site, allowing you to present data in an engaging and accessible manner. For example, a page can include announcements, document libraries, calendars, or external links.

Creating a New Page

To create a new page in SharePoint:

1. **Navigate to the Site Contents**

   o   Go to your SharePoint site and click on the **Settings Gear Icon** in the top-right corner.

   o   Select **Site Contents** from the dropdown menu.

2. **Choose the Pages Library**

   o   Locate the **Site Pages** library where all pages are stored.

   o   Click on **New** and select **Page** from the options.

3. **Select a Page Layout**

- o SharePoint offers a variety of pre-designed templates, including layouts for team collaboration, announcements, or custom designs.

- o Choose a template that aligns with your purpose, such as a blank page for customization or a news post for updates.

4. **Add Web Parts to Your Page**

- o Web parts are modular elements that you can drag and drop onto the page. Examples include:

  - **Text Editor**: Add formatted text content.

  - **Image or Video Embeds**: Display visual content to enhance the user experience.

  - **Document Library Web Part**: Showcase files stored in your site.

  - **Calendar Web Part**: Display events and schedules.

5. **Customize Your Page**

- o Adjust the layout by adding columns or resizing web parts.

- o Use the formatting toolbar to style text and visuals.

- o Hyperlink critical resources or include quick links for navigation.

6. **Save and Publish**

- o Click **Save as Draft** if the page is still under construction.

- o Once finalized, select **Publish** to make the page visible to your users.

Best Practices for Pages

- **Keep It Simple**: Avoid clutter and focus on presenting relevant information.

- **Use Visuals Wisely**: Add images or graphics to make content more engaging, but ensure they align with the site's theme.

- **Ensure Mobile Compatibility**: Preview your page to confirm it works well on mobile devices.

What Are Libraries in SharePoint?

Libraries in SharePoint are specialized repositories where documents, images, videos, or other files are stored and managed. They support collaboration by providing a centralized location for accessing and sharing files. Document libraries are the most commonly used type in SharePoint, but other options include picture libraries and asset libraries.

Creating a New Library

1. **Access the Site Contents**

   o   Navigate to **Settings > Site Contents**.

   o   Click **New > Document Library**.

2. **Name Your Library**

   o   Provide a descriptive name that reflects the content it will store, such as "Marketing Collateral" or "Project Documentation."

   o   Add an optional description to help users understand its purpose.

3. **Customize Library Settings**

   o   Enable version control to track changes to documents.

   o   Set permissions to define who can view, edit, or manage files.

   o   Configure metadata fields to organize content by categories such as project names, departments, or deadlines.

Adding Files to a Library

- **Drag-and-Drop Uploads**: Drag files directly into the library from your desktop.

- **Upload Button**: Use the **Upload** option to select individual files or folders.

- **Templates**: Create new files directly in the library using pre-configured templates (e.g., Word, Excel, PowerPoint).

Enhancing Libraries with Metadata and Views

Metadata and views transform libraries into powerful tools for content management.

- **Metadata**: Add custom columns (e.g., status, owner, or priority) to categorize documents.

- **Views**: Create filtered or sorted views to quickly access specific files. For example:

   o   A view for "Documents Updated This Week."

   o   A filtered view for files owned by specific team members.

Collaboration Features in Libraries

1. **Co-Authoring**:

   o Multiple users can work on a document simultaneously in real-time.

   o Changes are saved automatically, and version history allows you to revert edits if needed.

2. **Notifications**:

   o Set up alerts to receive updates when files are modified, deleted, or added.

3. **Integration with Microsoft Office**:

   o Open and edit files directly from the library in Office applications like Word or Excel.

Best Practices for Libraries

- **Organize with Folders**: Group files into folders to make navigation easier.

- **Use Consistent Naming Conventions**: Standardize file and folder names for clarity.

- **Apply Permissions Thoughtfully**: Restrict access to sensitive libraries as needed.

Conclusion

By effectively adding and managing pages and libraries in SharePoint, you can create a functional, visually appealing, and collaborative environment for your team. These tools not only enhance productivity but also simplify the way information is shared and accessed.

2.3.2 Organizing Content with Folders

Effective content organization is the backbone of a well-managed SharePoint site. When content is neatly arranged, it becomes easier for users to find what they need, collaborate efficiently, and maintain a productive workflow. In this section, we'll explore how folders can be utilized in SharePoint to create a logical and accessible structure for your site's content.

The Importance of Organizing Content

Content organization is not just about aesthetics; it's a critical factor that impacts usability, productivity, and overall site performance. Properly structured folders can:

- **Streamline Navigation**: Users can quickly locate documents without excessive searching.

- **Reduce Duplication**: A clear folder structure prevents the creation of redundant files.

- **Enhance Collaboration**: Team members can work cohesively when content is logically arranged.

- **Support Version Control**: Organized folders make it easier to track document history and updates.

Before diving into folder creation, it's essential to understand SharePoint's unique features, such as metadata, which can complement or even replace traditional folder structures.

Creating Folders in Document Libraries

Folders in SharePoint can be created within document libraries to help categorize content. Here's a step-by-step guide to setting up folders effectively:

1. **Navigate to the Document Library**:

   o Go to your SharePoint site and select the document library where you want to create folders.

2. **Access the New Folder Option**:

   o   Click the "+ New" button at the top of the library and select "Folder."

3. **Name Your Folder**:

   o   Assign a clear and descriptive name to the folder, such as "Project Plans" or "Marketing Materials." Avoid using vague or overly generic names.

4. **Set Folder Permissions (Optional)**:

   o   If specific access restrictions are required, configure folder-level permissions to control who can view or edit its contents.

5. **Add Subfolders as Needed**:

   o   Create subfolders within parent folders for further categorization. For example, under "Marketing Materials," you could have subfolders like "Campaigns" and "Assets."

Best Practices for Folder Naming and Structure

A consistent and logical folder structure is key to long-term usability. Follow these best practices when organizing content with folders:

- **Use a Hierarchical Approach**:

  Group related content under parent folders and use subfolders to add more detail.

  - Example: **Main Folder > Subfolder > Document.**

- **Stick to Simple Names**:

  Avoid special characters or overly lengthy names that could confuse users or lead to errors.

- **Adopt a Standard Naming Convention**:

  Ensure team members follow a consistent format, such as including dates, project codes, or department names.

  - Example: **2024_ProjectX_FinalReport.docx.**

- **Avoid Over-Nesting**:

  Excessive subfolder levels can make navigation cumbersome. Aim to keep folder structures no more than three levels deep.

Organizing Existing Content

If your SharePoint site already has content scattered across the library, reorganizing it can improve efficiency. Here's how:

1. **Audit Your Current Library**:

   - Identify redundant or outdated files. Archive or delete unnecessary content.

2. **Create a Folder Plan**:

   - Decide on the main categories and subcategories your folders will represent.

3. **Move Files into Folders**:

   - Drag and drop files into the appropriate folders. Alternatively, use the "Move To" option for batch processing.

4. **Update Links**:

o   If files are linked to other documents or pages, ensure links remain functional after moving them.

Using Metadata as an Alternative

While folders are intuitive for many users, SharePoint also supports metadata tagging as an alternative to traditional folder organization. Metadata allows you to assign keywords or categories to files, enabling advanced filtering and searching. For instance:

- Instead of a folder structure like **Department > Year > Project**, you can tag files with metadata fields such as **Department**, **Year**, and **Project Name**.

- Users can then sort and filter files dynamically without navigating through multiple folder layers.

Combining Folders and Metadata

In many cases, combining folders with metadata can provide the best of both worlds. For example:

- Use folders for broad categories like **Departments** or **Projects**.

- Apply metadata tags for finer details such as **Approval Status**, **Document Type**, or **Due Date**.

Collaborating with Folders

SharePoint folders are designed for teamwork. Here's how you can leverage folders for effective collaboration:

- **Shared Access**: Team members can access and edit files within shared folders, ensuring everyone is on the same page.

- **Notifications**: Enable alerts for folder changes to keep users informed of updates.

- **Version History**: SharePoint tracks changes made to documents within folders, allowing users to view or restore previous versions.

Troubleshooting Common Issues with Folders

Even with a well-organized structure, folder-related issues can arise. Below are common problems and their solutions:

- **Duplicate Folders**:

    o Problem: Multiple users create folders with similar names.

    o Solution: Implement a naming convention and educate users on its importance.

- **Access Denied Errors**:

    o Problem: Users are unable to access specific folders.

    o Solution: Check folder permissions and adjust them as needed.

- **Overlapping Content**:

    o Problem: Files are stored in multiple folders, leading to confusion.

    o Solution: Consolidate content and use metadata for cross-referencing.

Conclusion

Organizing content with folders in SharePoint is a fundamental practice that enhances usability and collaboration. By following best practices, leveraging metadata, and addressing potential issues proactively, you can create a streamlined and efficient content management system. Remember, the ultimate goal is to ensure that users can access the right information at the right time with minimal effort.

CHAPTER III
Document Management

3.1 Uploading and Storing Documents

Efficient document management is a cornerstone of SharePoint's functionality. The platform provides users with versatile tools to upload and store documents, making it easier for teams to access and collaborate on critical files. In this section, we'll delve into two primary methods of uploading documents to SharePoint: single uploads and bulk uploads. Understanding the differences and best practices for each will empower you to streamline your workflow and maximize productivity.

3.1.1 Single vs. Bulk Uploads

What Is a Single Upload?

A single upload is the process of uploading one document at a time to a SharePoint document library. This method is ideal for uploading individual files or when you need to carefully review and organize each file as you go. For example, if you are adding a finalized report to a specific folder in your document library, a single upload ensures precision in file placement and metadata tagging.

How to Perform a Single Upload

1. **Navigate to the Document Library**

   o   Open your SharePoint site and click on the document library where you want to upload the file.

2. **Click on the "Upload" Button**

o At the top of the library, locate and click the "Upload" button. This will open a file selection dialog.

3. **Choose the File**

   o Select the file from your computer that you want to upload.

4. **Add Metadata (Optional)**

   o Depending on the library settings, you may be prompted to fill in metadata fields such as title, author, or department.

5. **Confirm and Upload**

   o Click "Save" or "Upload" to add the document to the library.

Advantages of Single Uploads

- **Precision:** Allows you to carefully select and place each document.

- **Metadata Entry:** Facilitates accurate tagging of files during the upload process.

- **Immediate Review:** Gives you the opportunity to review the content and structure of the file before finalizing the upload.

Limitations of Single Uploads

- **Time-Consuming:** Uploading files one by one can be slow, especially for larger projects.

- **Not Ideal for Large Volumes:** If you have dozens or hundreds of files, single uploads can become impractical.

What Is a Bulk Upload?

Bulk uploading involves transferring multiple files or entire folders to a SharePoint document library at once. This method is designed for efficiency and is especially useful when onboarding a new project, migrating files from another system, or sharing a large set of related documents.

How to Perform a Bulk Upload

1. **Prepare Your Files**

    o Organize the files and folders you want to upload on your local drive. It's helpful to group them logically to maintain structure in SharePoint.

2. **Open the Document Library**

    o Go to the SharePoint library where you want to upload the files.

3. **Drag and Drop Files**

    o Simply drag the selected files or folders from your computer into the document library window in your browser. Alternatively, use the "Upload" button and select multiple files through the dialog box.

4. **Review and Confirm**

    o After the upload, review the files in the library to ensure they were transferred correctly.

Advanced Options for Bulk Uploads

- **Using OneDrive Sync:**

    o Sync your SharePoint library with your local OneDrive. Move files into the synced folder, and they will automatically upload to SharePoint.

- **PowerShell Scripts:**

    o For IT administrators, PowerShell scripts can automate bulk uploads, making it faster and easier to handle large migrations.

Advantages of Bulk Uploads

- **Efficiency:** Uploads large volumes of files in one go, saving time and effort.

- **Scalability:** Ideal for organizations handling substantial document migrations or updates.

- **Consistent Structure:** Allows you to maintain folder structures during the upload process.

Limitations of Bulk Uploads

- **Potential Errors:** Larger uploads may encounter connectivity issues or file limitations, such as unsupported file types or size restrictions.

- **Metadata Management:** Bulk uploads may bypass metadata fields unless predefined templates or automation tools are in place.

Best Practices for Uploading Documents

1. **Plan Before Uploading**

   o Organize files on your local system in a way that reflects the structure you want in SharePoint.

   o Decide whether you'll use folders, metadata, or a combination of both for organization.

2. **Check File Limitations**

   o SharePoint has limits on file sizes and types. Before uploading, ensure your files meet these requirements.

3. **Use Metadata for Bulk Uploads**

   o When uploading multiple files, use tools like Excel or Power Automate to batch-assign metadata fields to save time and maintain consistency.

4. **Ensure Permissions Are Set Correctly**

   o Verify that the library's permissions allow the intended users to access and edit the uploaded documents.

5. **Test and Validate After Uploading**

   o Once files are uploaded, test access, search functionality, and metadata tagging to ensure everything is working as expected.

Comparing Single vs. Bulk Uploads

Feature	Single Upload	Bulk Upload
Use Case	Small-scale, precise uploads	Large-scale, high-volume uploads
Speed	Slower	Faster
Metadata Assignment	Easier during upload	Requires post-upload adjustments
Best For	Individual files, sensitive data	Project migrations, team uploads

Both single and bulk uploads have their place in SharePoint workflows. Choosing the right method depends on your project's needs, the volume of files, and the level of organization required. By mastering these techniques, you'll ensure that your document management process is both efficient and effective.

3.1.2 Supported File Types

SharePoint is a versatile and robust platform designed to support a wide range of file types, making it a powerful tool for document management. Understanding the supported file types is essential for maximizing the efficiency of your workflows, ensuring compatibility, and avoiding potential issues when uploading or storing files. In this section, we will explore the types of files SharePoint supports, highlight common use cases for each, and discuss considerations for optimal file management.

Overview of Supported File Types

SharePoint supports most common file types used in business and collaboration. These include:

- **Document Files**: Microsoft Word (.doc, .docx), Excel (.xls, .xlsx), and PowerPoint (.ppt, .pptx) are the most frequently used formats, as SharePoint is seamlessly integrated with Microsoft Office.

- **PDF Files**: Portable Document Format (.pdf) files are universally supported and often used for sharing finalized documents or presentations.

- **Image Files**: SharePoint supports popular image formats such as JPEG (.jpg, .jpeg), PNG (.png), GIF (.gif), and BMP (.bmp). These are ideal for visual content like graphics, logos, or design files.

- **Video and Audio Files**: Video formats such as MP4 (.mp4) and audio formats like MP3 (.mp3) are supported, making SharePoint a useful repository for multimedia content.

- **Compressed Files**: SharePoint can store compressed file formats like ZIP (.zip) and RAR (.rar), which are often used to consolidate and share large sets of files.

- **Specialized Formats**: SharePoint also supports various other file types, including Visio files (.vsdx), OneNote files (.one), and InfoPath files (.xml).

File Size and Limitations

While SharePoint supports a wide variety of file types, there are specific file size limitations that users must adhere to:

- The maximum file size for uploads varies depending on the version of SharePoint and the configuration set by your administrator. For SharePoint Online, the default maximum is 250 GB per file.

- Large files may take longer to upload and sync, so it is recommended to compress or segment them if feasible.

Scenarios for File Compatibility

1. **Office Documents**
   These are the cornerstone of SharePoint's functionality, enabling real-time collaboration, version control, and seamless integration with Microsoft 365 apps. For example:

   o Team members can co-author a Word document stored in SharePoint while simultaneously adding comments.

   o Excel workbooks can be shared for data analysis or project tracking.

   o PowerPoint presentations can be uploaded and rehearsed in SharePoint's built-in presentation tools.

2. **PDF Files**

   PDF documents are widely used for sharing finalized reports, contracts, or manuals. SharePoint allows users to view PDFs directly within the platform without requiring external software.

    o   Use Case: A company handbook uploaded as a PDF can be easily accessed by all employees through a shared SharePoint library.

3. **Images and Multimedia Content**

SharePoint is not just for documents; it also supports multimedia, which is useful for marketing, training, and design teams.

    o   Use Case: A marketing team uploads product photos in JPEG format and promotional videos in MP4 to a centralized library for campaigns.

4. **Compressed Files**

SharePoint's ability to store ZIP and RAR files makes it convenient for sharing large file collections.

    o   Use Case: A project manager compresses project assets into a ZIP file and uploads it for team access.

Unsupported or Restricted File Types

While SharePoint is versatile, certain file types are blocked for security reasons, such as executable files (.exe) or script files (.js). These restrictions help prevent malicious activity and protect sensitive data.

- Administrators can adjust these settings to allow specific file types if necessary, but it is crucial to weigh the risks.

- Tip: Use SharePoint's metadata and tagging features to organize files instead of relying on potentially restricted extensions.

Best Practices for File Management

1. **Organize Files with Clear Naming Conventions**

    o   Use descriptive names to make files easy to locate. For example, instead of "Document1.pdf," use "2024-Q1-Financial-Report.pdf."

    o   Avoid using special characters that may cause issues during uploads.

2. **Leverage Metadata and Tags**

    o   Assign relevant metadata to files for better categorization. For instance, tag an image file as "Marketing" or "Product Launch 2024."

o   Use custom columns in document libraries to add context, such as "Department" or "Project Name."

3. **Monitor File Versions and Activity**

    o   SharePoint's versioning feature allows you to track changes and revert to previous versions if needed.

    o   Use audit logs to monitor file access and ensure compliance with organizational policies.

4. **Collaborate Securely**

    o   Set appropriate permissions to ensure files are accessible only to intended users.

    o   Use SharePoint's sharing features to grant or revoke access quickly.

Troubleshooting Common Issues

1. **File Upload Errors**

    o   Check file size limits and ensure the file format is supported.

    o   Verify your network connection and try uploading during non-peak hours if issues persist.

2. **File Compatibility Issues**

    o   For files created in older software versions, consider converting them to newer formats before uploading.

    o   Use SharePoint's built-in viewers for supported file types to avoid relying on external software.

3. **Managing Duplicate Files**

    o   Use SharePoint's duplicate detection tools to identify and consolidate redundant files.

By understanding the file types SharePoint supports and following best practices, you can effectively manage your documents, enhance collaboration, and maintain a well-organized digital workspace. SharePoint's flexibility and compatibility with diverse file types make it an indispensable tool for modern teams.

3.2 Working with Libraries

3.2.1 Creating Document Libraries

Document Libraries are one of the core components of SharePoint, designed to organize, store, and share documents within your organization. Creating and configuring document libraries effectively is essential for streamlining workflows and ensuring easy access to important files. This section provides a detailed guide to creating and setting up document libraries, tailored to meet your organization's unique needs.

What is a Document Library?

A document library is a specialized type of list in SharePoint that is optimized for storing documents and files. Unlike traditional folders, document libraries provide advanced features such as metadata, version control, and real-time collaboration. This makes them a powerful tool for managing and sharing information across teams.

Step-by-Step Guide to Creating a Document Library

1. Accessing the Site Where You Want to Create the Library

- Navigate to the SharePoint site where the library will reside.

- Ensure you have the necessary permissions (typically site owner or designer permissions).

2. Initiating the Creation of a New Document Library

- On the site's home page, click the "Settings" icon (gear icon) in the top-right corner.

- From the dropdown, select **Site Contents**.

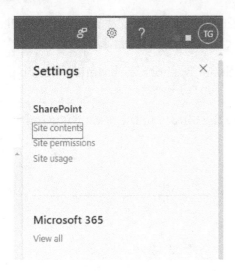

- Click on the **New** button and select **Document Library** from the menu.

3. Configuring the Library

- **Name Your Library**: Provide a descriptive and intuitive name that reflects its purpose (e.g., "Marketing Documents" or "Project Reports").

- **Add a Description**: Optionally, include a short description to help users understand the library's function.

- **Set Visibility**: Choose whether to show the library in the site's navigation for easy access.

4. Adding Columns to the Library

- SharePoint libraries support custom columns to store metadata.

- Click **Add column** to create columns such as "Document Type," "Review Date," or "Owner."

- Select the type of column (e.g., text, date, dropdown) based on the metadata you want to capture.

5. Customizing Views

- By default, SharePoint provides a standard view, but you can customize it to suit your team's needs.

- Use the **Edit Current View** option to define how documents appear, such as sorting by "Last Modified" or grouping by "Department."

6. Finalizing the Setup

- Once the library is created and configured, test its functionality by uploading a few sample documents.

- Ensure that team members can access, upload, and collaborate as intended.

Best Practices for Creating Document Libraries

1. Use Descriptive Names and Consistent Naming Conventions

- The library's name should clearly indicate its purpose.

- Establish a naming convention for folders and files to maintain consistency across the library.

2. Leverage Metadata Over Folders

- Metadata allows you to categorize and filter documents without creating deep folder structures.

- This approach reduces complexity and enhances searchability.

3. Define User Permissions Thoughtfully

- Assign permissions based on roles and responsibilities. For instance:

  o Full Control: Site owners and administrators.

  o Contribute: Team members who need to upload or edit documents.

  o Read: Users who only need viewing access.

4. Enable Version Control

- Activate versioning in the library settings to maintain a history of changes to documents.

- This is particularly useful for tracking edits and restoring previous versions if needed.

5. Plan for Scalability

- Anticipate growth in the volume of documents and users.

- Regularly review and reorganize the library to avoid clutter and ensure optimal performance.

Benefits of Creating a Well-Structured Document Library

1. **Enhanced Collaboration**

   o A centralized location for files fosters better communication and teamwork.

   o Users can co-author documents and track changes in real time.

2. **Improved Accessibility**

   o Search features and metadata make it easy to locate specific documents, even in large libraries.

3. **Increased Productivity**

   o A well-organized library reduces time spent searching for files, allowing teams to focus on their tasks.

4. **Data Security and Compliance**

- o SharePoint's built-in security features protect sensitive information.

- o Document libraries can be configured to meet regulatory compliance standards.

5. **Seamless Integration**

- o Document libraries integrate with other Microsoft 365 tools like Teams, Word, and Power Automate, enhancing workflows.

Common Challenges and How to Address Them

1. Overloading Folders with Files

- **Problem**: Deep folder structures can make navigation cumbersome.

- **Solution**: Rely on metadata and views to organize documents logically.

2. Conflicting Permissions

- **Problem**: Users may accidentally gain access to files they shouldn't see.

- **Solution**: Regularly audit and adjust permissions to align with team requirements.

3. Document Duplication

- **Problem**: Multiple versions of the same file can clutter the library.

- **Solution**: Encourage the use of check-in/check-out features and educate users on version control.

Example Use Cases for Document Libraries

1. Project Management

- Store project plans, timelines, and deliverables in a single library.

- Use metadata to categorize documents by project phase or team.

2. Knowledge Base

- Create a library for storing FAQs, policies, and training materials.

- Configure the library to display the most frequently accessed documents prominently.

3. Client Collaboration

- Set up a dedicated library for each client to share contracts, reports, and presentations securely.

- Enable external sharing with appropriate permissions.

Conclusion

Creating a document library in SharePoint is a foundational skill that sets the stage for effective document management. By following the steps outlined in this section and adhering to best practices, you can build libraries that empower your team to work efficiently and collaboratively. As you gain experience, explore advanced features like workflows, automation, and integration with other Microsoft tools to unlock SharePoint's full potential.

3.2.2 Version Control in SharePoint

Version control is one of the most powerful features of SharePoint, enabling teams to track changes, maintain records of document iterations, and collaborate more effectively. By understanding and leveraging version control, users can prevent data loss, ensure accountability, and foster better team collaboration. This section will provide a comprehensive guide to using version control in SharePoint.

Understanding Version Control

Version control in SharePoint allows users to manage changes to documents by automatically saving and organizing multiple versions of a file. This feature enables teams to view a document's history, restore previous versions if necessary, and understand who made specific changes.

- **Major Versions vs. Minor Versions**: SharePoint distinguishes between major and minor versions. Major versions represent significant updates (e.g., "1.0," "2.0"), while minor versions track smaller, incremental changes (e.g., "1.1," "1.2").

- **Automatic vs. Manual Saving**: SharePoint's version control system works automatically when users save changes, ensuring no edits are overlooked. However, manual versioning settings can also be configured to align with specific team workflows.

Enabling Version Control in Document Libraries

To use version control effectively, administrators or site owners need to enable it for specific document libraries. Here's a step-by-step guide:

1. **Access the Library Settings**:

    o   Navigate to the document library where you want to enable version control.

    o   Click on the gear icon in the upper-right corner, then select *Library Settings*.

2. **Configure Versioning Settings**:

    o   In the Library Settings menu, click on *Versioning Settings*.

    o   Choose the desired versioning method:

        ▪   **Major Versions Only**: Suitable for teams focusing on significant updates.

        ▪   **Major and Minor Versions**: Ideal for detailed tracking during collaborative work.

3. **Set Limits on Versions**:

    o   SharePoint allows administrators to limit the number of versions stored to conserve space. For example, you can retain the latest 50 versions and delete older ones.

4. **Save the Settings**:

   o   Click *OK* to confirm your changes, and the library will start tracking document versions moving forward.

Viewing Version History

Once version control is enabled, users can access the history of a document to see who made changes and when.

1. **Access Version History**:

   o   Hover over the file name in the document library.

   o   Click the ellipsis (...) or right-click the file and select *Version History*.

2. **Understanding the History Pane**:

   o   A panel will appear displaying all versions of the file, listed in reverse chronological order.

   o   Each entry includes the version number, the date and time of modification, the editor's name, and optional comments (if added during the save process).

3. **Restore or View Versions**:

   o   Select a version to view its content or click *Restore* to replace the current version with an earlier one. Restoring does not delete the current version but instead creates a new version based on the restored content.

Best Practices for Version Control

To maximize the benefits of version control, teams should follow these best practices:

1. **Use Comments When Saving**:

   o   Encourage team members to add comments when saving changes, describing what they modified. This practice simplifies the review process and provides context for future reference.

2. **Train Team Members**:

o   Ensure all users understand how to access and manage version history. Conduct regular training sessions or provide documentation to avoid confusion.

3. **Review Old Versions Regularly**:

    o   Periodically review and clean up old versions to optimize storage space while maintaining essential records.

4. **Integrate with Workflows**:

    o   Combine version control with SharePoint workflows to automate approval processes and streamline document management.

Troubleshooting Version Control Issues

While SharePoint's version control system is robust, occasional issues may arise:

1. **Missing Versions**:

    o   If older versions seem to disappear, check the version limits set in the library settings. Increasing the retention limit may resolve the issue.

2. **Conflicts During Co-Authoring**:

    o   When multiple users edit the same document simultaneously, version conflicts can occur. SharePoint typically creates a separate copy for conflicting edits, which users must manually reconcile.

3. **Permission Restrictions**:

    o   Users with limited permissions may be unable to view or restore certain versions. Ensure appropriate permissions are assigned to team members.

Advanced Features in Version Control

1. **Approval Workflows**:

    o   Pairing version control with approval workflows ensures that only reviewed and approved versions are published as major versions. This feature is particularly useful in regulated industries.

2. **Integration with Microsoft Office Applications**:

   o   When working in applications like Word or Excel, users can access version history directly from the *File* menu. This seamless integration enhances usability and speeds up version-related tasks.

3. **Using Power Automate for Version Management**:

   o   Automate repetitive tasks related to versioning, such as sending notifications when a new major version is published or archiving older versions based on predefined criteria.

Case Study: Version Control in Action

Imagine a marketing team collaborating on a product brochure:

- A draft is uploaded to the SharePoint library, and version control is enabled.

- Each team member edits the document, saving their changes with comments like "Updated pricing details" or "Revised layout."

- After several revisions, the manager reviews the version history, restores an earlier version that aligns with brand guidelines, and publishes it as the final version.

Through SharePoint's version control, the team avoids confusion, tracks accountability, and ensures a polished final product.

By mastering version control, teams can enhance their collaboration, maintain organized records, and simplify document management within SharePoint.

3.3 Collaborating on Documents

3.3.1 Co-Authoring in Real-Time

Collaboration has become a cornerstone of modern workplaces, and SharePoint's co-authoring feature is a game-changer for teams working on shared documents. This functionality allows multiple users to simultaneously edit documents, fostering a more dynamic and efficient workflow. In this section, we will explore how co-authoring works, its benefits, tips for effective usage, and common challenges to avoid.

Understanding Real-Time Co-Authoring

Real-time co-authoring in SharePoint enables team members to work on Word, Excel, PowerPoint, and other Office documents together without locking each other out of the file. Edits appear almost instantly, with each contributor's changes highlighted for clarity. Whether you're in the same office or spread across different time zones, SharePoint ensures that your team stays in sync.

To use co-authoring:

- **Ensure Compatibility:** The document must be stored in a SharePoint library or OneDrive for Business. Supported file formats include .docx, .xlsx, and .pptx.

- **Open in the Right Application:** Use Microsoft 365 apps (desktop or online) for the best co-authoring experience. Older versions of Office may not support this feature.

- **Share the Document:** Grant the appropriate permissions to collaborators. Anyone with edit access can co-author.

Benefits of Real-Time Co-Authoring

1. **Enhanced Productivity:** Teams can draft, review, and finalize documents faster, as everyone works together instead of waiting for individual edits.

2. **Improved Transparency:** Changes are visible to all contributors in real-time, reducing misunderstandings and redundant edits.

3. **Seamless Integration:** Co-authoring integrates with other Microsoft tools, such as Teams and Outlook, making collaboration even more cohesive.

4. **Version History:** SharePoint automatically saves and tracks changes, allowing you to revert to earlier versions if needed.

How to Enable and Use Co-Authoring

- **Upload the Document to SharePoint:** Start by uploading the document to a shared library in SharePoint. Ensure that the document resides in a folder with proper edit permissions.

- **Invite Collaborators:** Use the "Share" button to invite team members. You can send invitations directly through email or copy a shareable link.

- **Open and Edit Together:** Collaborators can open the document in their browser or Microsoft 365 apps. Each person's presence is indicated by a colored cursor or marker.

- **Communicate Changes:** Use the built-in comments feature or pair co-authoring with Microsoft Teams for discussions.

Best Practices for Co-Authoring

- **Establish Guidelines:** Define roles and responsibilities for contributors to avoid overlap or conflicting edits.

- **Use Comments Effectively:** Encourage team members to use comments for feedback instead of making uncoordinated changes.

- **Enable Version Control:** Always keep track of changes using SharePoint's version history feature.

- **Check Permissions:** Regularly review who has access to the document to prevent unauthorized changes.

- **Minimize Overload:** Limit the number of simultaneous editors for large or complex documents to avoid confusion.

Integrating with Other Collaboration Tools

Combine SharePoint's co-authoring capabilities with other Microsoft tools to create a seamless workflow:

- **Microsoft Teams:** Use Teams to chat or call while co-authoring for real-time communication.

- **Outlook Integration:** Share document links in emails for quick access and updates.

- **Power Automate:** Automate notifications for edits or approvals when certain changes are made.

Troubleshooting Common Issues

Despite its robust design, co-authoring can sometimes face challenges. Here are some common issues and solutions:

1. **Conflicts in Edits:**
    1. **Cause:** Two users edit the same part of the document simultaneously.
    2. **Solution:** Resolve conflicts using the desktop version of the Office app, which highlights overlapping edits.

2. **Connectivity Problems:**
    1. **Cause:** Poor internet connection or syncing delays.
    2. **Solution:** Ensure stable internet access and refresh the document to sync changes.

3. **Unsupported Features:**
    1. **Cause:** Some advanced features in Office desktop apps aren't supported in the browser version.
    2. **Solution:** Use the desktop application for full functionality when necessary.

4. **Permission Errors:**
    1. **Cause:** A user without edit permissions attempts to make changes.

2. **Solution:** Verify and update user permissions in the SharePoint settings.

Real-World Applications of Co-Authoring

- **Collaborative Reporting:** Teams can draft annual reports, business plans, or project summaries in real-time, ensuring consistency and faster turnaround.

- **Joint Proposals:** Cross-departmental teams can work on proposals or bids without the hassle of managing multiple document versions.

- **Training Materials:** Trainers and subject matter experts can collaboratively develop and refine educational content.

- **Data Analysis:** Teams working on Excel can co-author complex spreadsheets, updating data and formulas collaboratively.

Conclusion

Co-authoring in SharePoint exemplifies modern workplace collaboration. By enabling teams to work on the same document simultaneously, it eliminates inefficiencies and fosters a culture of transparency and teamwork. When used effectively, co-authoring becomes a powerful tool for enhancing productivity, driving innovation, and achieving organizational goals.

With the tips and practices shared in this section, you're now equipped to leverage SharePoint's co-authoring capabilities to their fullest potential. Whether you're drafting documents, analyzing data, or creating presentations, SharePoint ensures your team is always on the same page—literally.

3.3.2 Using Comments and Notifications

Efficient collaboration in SharePoint extends beyond sharing documents and editing them in real time. The use of comments and notifications is an integral part of fostering communication and feedback, ensuring everyone involved stays informed and aligned on progress. This section explores how to effectively use these tools to streamline teamwork and enhance productivity.

Leveraging Comments for Feedback and Discussion

Comments in SharePoint provide a straightforward way for team members to share insights, ask questions, and offer feedback directly within a document or file. By keeping conversations contextually linked to the specific content, teams can reduce confusion and centralize discussions.

Where to Add Comments

SharePoint's commenting feature is accessible across various file types, including Word documents, Excel spreadsheets, and PowerPoint presentations stored in libraries. To add a comment:

Open the file directly in the online viewer or the respective desktop application integrated with SharePoint.

Highlight the specific text, cell, or slide where feedback is required.

Select **"New Comment"** or a similar option to attach the comment to the selected content.

Best Practices for Writing Effective Comments

- **Be Specific**: Reference the exact section or detail needing attention.

- **Provide Constructive Feedback**: Instead of vague remarks like "needs improvement," offer actionable suggestions such as "Consider rephrasing this sentence for clarity."

- **Stay Professional and Courteous**: Comments should foster collaboration, not conflict.

Managing and Resolving Comments

Once comments are added, they can be addressed directly in the document. SharePoint allows users to:

- Reply to existing comments for clarity or additional discussion.

- Mark comments as resolved once the necessary changes have been made, keeping the conversation tidy and up-to-date.

- Delete outdated or irrelevant comments if necessary, ensuring the document remains uncluttered.

Utilizing Notifications for Seamless Updates

Notifications in SharePoint are designed to keep team members informed about changes, comments, and other actions in a document. Properly configuring notifications ensures that everyone stays updated without the need for constant manual checks.

Setting Up Alerts

Alerts are one of SharePoint's most robust notification tools. Users can configure alerts for specific files, folders, or libraries to receive updates via email or SMS when:

- A document is edited.

- A new comment is added.

- A file is moved, renamed, or deleted.

To set up an alert:

> Navigate to the document library or file where you want notifications.
>
> Click on the **"Alert Me"** button, usually found in the toolbar.
>
> Customize the alert settings by choosing the event type, frequency (instant, daily, or weekly summaries), and recipients.

Integrating with Microsoft Teams for Real-Time Notifications

For teams using Microsoft Teams alongside SharePoint, notifications can be seamlessly integrated. By linking a SharePoint library to a Teams channel, members can receive real-time alerts directly in the chat interface, enabling faster responses and collaboration.

Notification Etiquette

While notifications are helpful, overusing them can lead to notification fatigue. To optimize their impact:

- Only enable alerts for critical changes or high-priority documents.

- Group updates into daily or weekly summaries for non-urgent tasks.

- Encourage team members to check their SharePoint activity feed regularly for non-critical updates.

Collaborating Across Teams with Comments and Notifications

SharePoint is particularly powerful for cross-departmental collaboration, where comments and notifications can bridge communication gaps. For instance:

- **Project Management**: Managers can use comments to gather feedback on project plans while notifications keep stakeholders informed about deadlines and changes.

- **Marketing and Creative Teams**: Designers and writers can exchange ideas and revisions within the file itself, reducing reliance on lengthy email chains.

- **Client-Facing Collaboration**: When working with external stakeholders, comments provide a transparent way to address feedback, while notifications keep clients updated on progress.

Common Challenges and Solutions

Despite their benefits, using comments and notifications effectively requires addressing some common challenges:

Challenge 1: Overwhelming Number of Comments

- **Solution**: Assign a team member to periodically review and summarize comments, creating a clear action list.

Challenge 2: Missed Notifications

- **Solution**: Encourage team members to check their SharePoint activity feeds and configure alerts appropriately for high-priority items.

Challenge 3: Lack of Context in Comments

- **Solution**: Establish team guidelines for comments, emphasizing clarity and specificity.

Advanced Features for Enhanced Collaboration

To take full advantage of SharePoint's collaboration tools, consider leveraging these advanced features:

1. **Mentions in Comments**: Use the "@mention" feature to tag specific team members, ensuring they're notified about relevant feedback.

2. **Automated Workflows**: Combine notifications with Power Automate to trigger reminders or approvals based on document updates.

3. **Comment Analytics**: Use third-party tools to analyze comment trends, identifying common areas of discussion or bottlenecks in the review process.

By mastering comments and notifications, teams can significantly enhance their collaborative efforts in SharePoint. These tools not only centralize feedback and streamline updates but also create a more connected and efficient workflow, empowering teams to work smarter and achieve their goals more effectively.

CHAPTER IV
Lists and Libraries

4.1 Introduction to Lists and Libraries

4.1.1 Key Differences and Use Cases

In SharePoint, **lists** and **libraries** are two foundational elements that serve as the backbone of content organization, management, and collaboration. Understanding their differences and specific use cases is essential for maximizing productivity and creating efficient workflows in your SharePoint environment.

Understanding Lists in SharePoint

A **list** in SharePoint is a structured collection of data, similar to a table in a database or a spreadsheet. It is used to organize and manage information in rows and columns, where each row represents a record and each column represents a specific field or attribute of that record. Lists are incredibly versatile and can be customized with various fields, views, and rules to suit the needs of your team or project.

Common Features of Lists:

- **Custom Columns**: Add fields for text, numbers, dates, choice menus, or even lookups from other lists.

- **Views**: Create personalized or team-wide views to filter and sort data based on specific criteria.

- **Integration with Power Automate**: Automate tasks like sending reminders or updating statuses.

- **Version History**: Keep track of changes to list items over time.

- **Attachments**: Optionally include files or documents related to a specific record.

Understanding Libraries in SharePoint

A **library** in SharePoint is designed specifically for storing and managing files. While it shares some similarities with lists, such as the ability to create views or add metadata, libraries are tailored for documents, images, videos, and other file types. Libraries excel in enabling collaboration, maintaining version history, and integrating with Office applications for seamless file editing.

Common Features of Libraries:

- **Version Control**: Automatically save previous versions of files for reference or rollback.

- **Check-In and Check-Out**: Lock files while they are being edited to prevent conflicts.

- **Metadata**: Add custom fields to categorize and organize files.

- **Preview and Edit**: View file previews directly in SharePoint or edit them in Office apps without downloading.

- **Document Sets**: Group related files together into a single entity for streamlined management.

Key Differences Between Lists and Libraries

Feature/Capability	Lists	Libraries
Primary Purpose	Managing structured data (rows and columns).	Storing and managing files.
Data Type	Items with fields like text, numbers, dates.	Files such as Word documents, PDFs, images.
Attachments	Supported but secondary.	Core functionality—files are the main focus.
Version History	Available for items.	Robust versioning for files.
Integration with Office Apps	Limited.	Deep integration for editing and collaboration.

For example, if you are tracking **employee tasks**, a list would be ideal as it allows you to add details like due dates, priority levels, and assignees. On the other hand, if you need a repository for project-related documents like proposals, contracts, and blueprints, a library is the right choice.

Use Cases for Lists

1. **Task Management**

   o Track tasks for team projects, with columns for task name, due date, priority, and status.

   o Use workflows to send reminders or update task statuses automatically.

2. **Customer Information**

   o Maintain a client database, complete with columns for names, email addresses, phone numbers, and sales data.

3. **Issue Tracking**

   o Log and monitor issues with detailed fields for issue description, assigned team member, and resolution status.

4. **Event Planning**

   o Create a list for event registrations, including fields for attendee names, contact details, and special requests.

Use Cases for Libraries

1. **Document Management**

   o Store project documents, ensuring all team members have access to the latest versions.

   o Use metadata to categorize documents by type, such as "Contracts," "Proposals," or "Reports."

2. **Media Repository**

   o Organize high-resolution images, videos, or audio files for marketing campaigns.

- o Leverage SharePoint's preview capabilities to review media without downloading.

3. **Policy and Procedure Manuals**

- o Host organizational guidelines and procedures with version history to track updates.

- o Ensure compliance by setting permissions for specific user groups.

4. **Team Collaboration**

- o Enable multiple team members to co-author presentations or reports in real time.

- o Track changes and comments for a transparent editing process.

Choosing the Right Tool for the Job

When deciding between a list and a library, consider the type of data you are working with and the functionality required.

- Use a **list** when your goal is to manage structured data, such as inventories, employee directories, or surveys.

- Opt for a **library** when working with files that require collaborative editing, such as team documents or design assets.

Benefits of Combining Lists and Libraries

In many scenarios, the most efficient approach is to combine both tools. For instance:

- Use a **list** to track the status of tasks and deadlines.

- Link those tasks to relevant documents stored in a **library**, providing easy access to supporting files.

By leveraging the strengths of both lists and libraries, you can create robust workflows that optimize efficiency and team collaboration.

This comprehensive understanding of the key differences and use cases between lists and libraries will set the foundation for effectively managing and organizing content in SharePoint. In the following sections, we will delve deeper into how to create, manage, and optimize these tools to meet your specific needs.

4.1.2 Popular Templates for Lists

SharePoint offers a range of templates for creating lists, each designed to meet specific business needs and streamline operations. Whether you are tracking tasks, managing assets, or storing customer information, these templates provide a versatile foundation for building an efficient and user-friendly system. Below, we will explore some of the most popular templates, their features, and how they can be tailored to suit your organization's requirements.

1. Task List

The **Task List** template is ideal for project management and activity tracking. It allows you to create, assign, and monitor tasks efficiently. Key features include:

- **Columns for Task Details:** Fields for due dates, assignees, priority levels, and progress percentages.

- **Gantt Chart View:** A visual representation of tasks along a timeline, aiding in planning and resource allocation.

- **Integration with Microsoft Planner:** Tasks can sync with Planner for advanced collaboration.

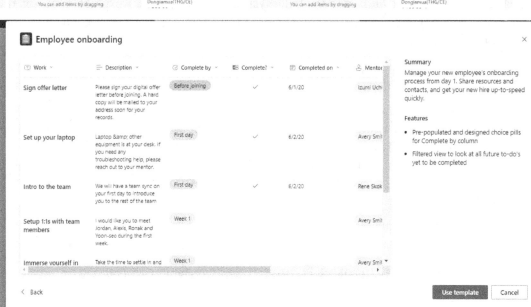

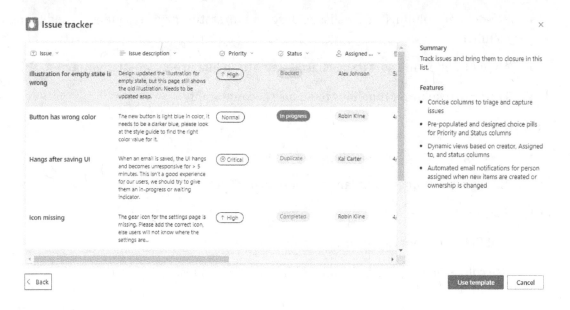

Use Cases:

- Managing team deliverables for projects.

- Tracking individual assignments in academic or corporate environments.

Customization Tips:

- Add columns for estimated time to completion or dependency links to create a more comprehensive task management system.

- Set up automated notifications for overdue tasks using Power Automate.

2. Issue Tracking List

The **Issue Tracking List** is designed to log and monitor issues within a project or operation. This template is widely used in IT and customer service settings to document and resolve problems.

Key Features:

- Pre-defined columns such as issue description, status, priority, and assigned team members.

- Ability to filter and sort issues based on criteria like urgency or assignment.

- Tracking resolution timelines to ensure accountability.

Use Cases:

- Logging software bugs during development.

- Managing customer complaints or support tickets.

Customization Tips:

- Add fields for root cause analysis and resolution time.

- Use color-coded views to highlight high-priority issues.

---

3. Calendar List

The **Calendar List** template supports scheduling and time management. It functions as an interactive calendar where you can log events, appointments, and deadlines.

Key Features:

- Monthly, weekly, and daily views.

- Event details such as location, attendees, and recurring options.

- Integration with Outlook for centralized scheduling.

Use Cases:

- Planning team meetings, company holidays, or product launches.

- Coordinating shared resources like meeting rooms.

Customization Tips:

- Overlay multiple calendars to view different departments' schedules simultaneously.

- Enable email reminders for upcoming events.

4. Contacts List

The **Contacts List** template is a straightforward tool for storing and organizing contact information. It acts as a lightweight CRM solution for teams that need basic contact management.

Key Features:

- Fields for name, phone number, email address, and company.
- Easy import/export to Excel for bulk updates.
- Permissions settings to control access to sensitive data.

Use Cases:

- Maintaining vendor and supplier databases.
- Creating a directory of team members or clients.

Customization Tips:

- Add custom fields for social media profiles or preferred communication methods.
- Create filtered views for regional or departmental contact lists.

5. Custom List

The **Custom List** is perhaps the most versatile template in SharePoint. It provides a blank slate that allows users to define their own structure and fields, making it suitable for any scenario not covered by default templates.

Key Features:

- Fully customizable columns to match unique data requirements.
- Compatibility with workflows and Power Automate.
- Dynamic views for filtering, grouping, or summarizing data.

Use Cases:

- Tracking employee training and certifications.

- Creating an inventory of office supplies or assets.

Customization Tips:

- Use calculated columns for real-time data analysis (e.g., calculating totals or durations).

- Combine with Power Apps to build a user-friendly interface for data entry.

6. Survey List

The **Survey List** template enables you to create questionnaires and gather feedback from users. This is a valuable tool for collecting insights to improve processes, products, or employee satisfaction.

Key Features:

- Support for multiple question types, including text, choice, and ratings.

- Analytics tools for summarizing survey results.

- Option to make surveys anonymous for honest feedback.

Use Cases:

- Conducting employee satisfaction surveys.

- Gathering feedback after events or training sessions.

Customization Tips:

- Use branching logic to guide respondents through relevant questions.

- Export survey results to Excel for detailed analysis.

7. Asset Tracking List

The **Asset Tracking List** is specifically designed for monitoring company assets, such as equipment, software licenses, or vehicles.

Key Features:

- Pre-configured fields for asset type, location, and maintenance schedule.

- Integration with barcode scanning apps for easier inventory updates.

- Automated reminders for upcoming maintenance or warranty expirations.

Use Cases:

- Managing office equipment like laptops or printers.

- Tracking field assets such as company vehicles.

Customization Tips:

- Add images to each asset for better identification.

- Include fields for financial details, such as purchase price and depreciation.

8. Announcements List

The **Announcements List** is perfect for sharing updates and important news with your team or organization.

Key Features:

- A simple structure for title, body text, and expiration date.

- Visibility on the SharePoint homepage or in specific team sites.

Use Cases:

- Posting HR updates, such as new hires or policy changes.

- Sharing departmental news or upcoming deadlines.

Customization Tips:

- Categorize announcements by department for better organization.

- Enable notifications to inform team members when new announcements are posted.

Choosing the Right Template for Your Needs

Selecting the right template depends on your organization's unique workflows and objectives. While templates like Task Lists and Issue Tracking Lists are highly specialized, options like Custom Lists provide unmatched flexibility for innovative solutions.

By understanding the core features and capabilities of each template, you can maximize SharePoint's potential and create a more productive, collaborative environment. The next section will dive into creating and managing lists to help you make the most of these templates.

4.2 Creating and Managing Lists

4.2.1 Customizing Columns and Views

Lists in SharePoint are one of its most versatile features, providing a powerful way to organize, track, and share information across teams. Customizing columns and views is essential for tailoring a list to meet your specific needs, whether you're tracking project tasks, managing contacts, or collecting customer feedback. In this section, we will explore how to create and modify columns, customize views, and leverage these features for improved productivity and collaboration.

Understanding Columns in SharePoint Lists

Columns are the building blocks of a SharePoint list, defining the type of data that can be entered and how it is formatted. Each column serves as a field in your list, such as "Name," "Due Date," or "Priority." By customizing columns, you can ensure the list captures the exact data you need while maintaining consistency and clarity.

Types of Columns

SharePoint offers a variety of column types to suit different data requirements:

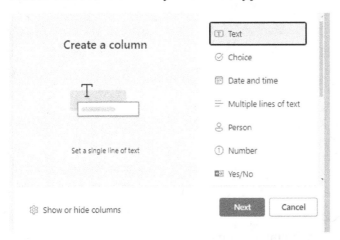

1. **Single Line of Text**: For short, single-line entries like names or titles.

2. **Multiple Lines of Text**: For longer descriptions or notes.

3. **Number**: For numerical data like quantities or percentages.

4. **Date and Time**: For scheduling deadlines or event dates.

5. **Choice**: For predefined options, such as status or categories.

6. **Lookup**: To pull data from another list in SharePoint.

7. **Person or Group**: To assign tasks or indicate ownership.

8. **Yes/No (Checkbox)**: For simple true/false data.

Adding a New Column

To add a column to your list:

1. Open the desired list in SharePoint.

2. Click **+ Add Column** at the top of the list.

3. Select the desired column type from the dropdown menu.

4. Enter a name and, if applicable, additional settings such as default values, required fields, or validation rules.

5. Click **Save** to apply your changes.

Customizing Column Settings

Each column type has its unique settings to enhance functionality:

- **Choice Column**: Define the list of selectable options, enable multiple selections, or display choices as a dropdown or checkboxes.

- **Date Column**: Configure date format and decide whether to include time.

- **Number Column**: Set a minimum and maximum value range, specify decimal places, or include a default value.

Enhancing Usability with Calculated Columns

Calculated columns allow you to derive new data based on other columns in your list. For example:

- Automatically calculate task completion dates by adding a specific number of days to the start date.

- Concatenate values from two columns to create a unique identifier.

To create a calculated column:

1. Add a new column and choose **Calculated (calculation based on other columns)** as the type.

2. Enter your formula in the provided field. SharePoint supports common mathematical, logical, and text functions.

3. Specify the data type for the result, such as text or number.

4. Save your settings to see the calculated results in your list.

Customizing Views

While columns determine the data stored in a list, views define how that data is displayed. SharePoint views allow you to filter, sort, group, and format list items, ensuring the most relevant information is presented at a glance.

Types of Views

1. **Standard View**: A traditional table layout.

2. **Calendar View**: Displays date-based information on a calendar grid.

3. **Gallery View**: Shows items as cards with visual emphasis.

4. **Datasheet View**: A grid-based view resembling a spreadsheet.

Creating a Custom View

To create a new view:

1. Open the list and click **All Items** in the view selector dropdown.

2. Select **Create New View**.

3. Choose the type of view (e.g., Standard, Calendar) and give it a name.

4. Configure filters, sorting, and grouping settings to display the desired data.

5. Save your view for future use.

Configuring View Filters and Sorts

- **Filters**: Narrow down list items based on specific criteria, such as showing only tasks assigned to you.

- **Sorting**: Arrange items by column values in ascending or descending order, such as sorting tasks by priority or due date.

Grouping Data

SharePoint allows you to group list items by column values, creating a collapsible hierarchy:

1. In the view settings, enable grouping.

2. Select a column to group by, such as "Project Name" or "Status."

3. Optionally, add a second-level grouping for deeper categorization.

Using Conditional Formatting in Views

Conditional formatting highlights specific list items based on rules you define. For instance, overdue tasks can be displayed in red, or high-priority items in bold.

To apply conditional formatting:

1. Open the list, go to the view you want to customize, and click **Format Current View**.

2. Select **Conditional Formatting** and define your rules using JSON code or pre-configured templates.

3. Save your changes to see the updated visual cues.

Tips for Optimizing Columns and Views

1. **Minimize Clutter**: Avoid adding too many columns or excessive details in a single view. Use multiple views to manage data effectively.

2. **Leverage Templates**: Use existing SharePoint templates to save time and maintain consistency.

3. **Train Users**: Ensure team members understand how to utilize views to access the information they need.

4. **Review Regularly**: Periodically review columns and views to ensure they align with evolving project requirements.

Customizing columns and views transforms a generic SharePoint list into a tailored solution that fits your team's needs, enhancing usability, and ensuring your data is organized, accessible, and actionable.

4.2.2 Automating Processes with Workflows

Automating processes within SharePoint lists using workflows is one of the most powerful features of the platform. By leveraging workflows, organizations can streamline repetitive tasks, ensure consistency, and reduce manual errors, all while increasing efficiency. This section will guide you through the basics of workflows in SharePoint, their practical applications, and how to create and manage them effectively.

Understanding Workflows in SharePoint

Workflows are automated sequences of actions that perform tasks based on predefined conditions. These can range from simple actions, such as sending an email notification when an item is added to a list, to complex multi-step processes involving conditional logic, approvals, and integrations with external tools.

SharePoint provides several out-of-the-box workflows, including:

- **Approval Workflows**: Route items for review and approval.

- **Feedback Workflows**: Collect and consolidate feedback on documents or list items.

- **Three-State Workflows**: Track the progress of an item through three distinct states (e.g., Not Started, In Progress, Completed).

Additionally, SharePoint integrates with Power Automate, allowing you to create custom workflows tailored to specific business needs.

Benefits of Workflow Automation

Automating processes in SharePoint lists provides several key advantages:

1. **Consistency**: Ensures processes are followed the same way every time.

2. **Time Savings**: Reduces the time spent on repetitive, manual tasks.

3. **Error Reduction**: Minimizes human errors by automating data handling and notifications.

4. **Scalability**: Easily adapt workflows to accommodate increased workloads or organizational growth.

5. **Improved Collaboration**: Enhances communication by automatically notifying relevant stakeholders.

Getting Started with Workflows

To create workflows for your SharePoint lists, follow these steps:

1. Identify the Process to Automate

Begin by analyzing the task or process you want to automate. Identify the key steps, decision points, and stakeholders involved. For example, if your process involves task assignments, you might want the workflow to automatically assign tasks to team members and send reminders if deadlines are missed.

2. Choose a Workflow Tool

SharePoint offers two primary tools for creating workflows:

- **Built-In Workflows**: Predefined templates that cover common scenarios, such as approvals.

- **Power Automate**: A more advanced tool that enables custom workflow creation with drag-and-drop functionality and integration with other Microsoft 365 apps.

3. Configure the Workflow

Once you've chosen a tool, you can configure the workflow by defining triggers, actions, and conditions. For instance:

- **Trigger**: An event that starts the workflow, such as a new item being added to the list.

- **Action**: The task the workflow performs, such as sending an email.

- **Condition**: Rules that dictate when specific actions occur, such as "if status equals 'Approved,' then notify the manager."

Example: Automating a Task Approval Workflow

Let's create a basic workflow for automating task approvals using Power Automate:

Step 1: Create a SharePoint List

Set up a list to track tasks. Include columns like:

- **Task Name** (Text)

- **Assigned To** (Person/Group)

- **Due Date** (Date)

- **Status** (Choice: Pending, Approved, Rejected)

Step 2: Access Power Automate

- Navigate to your SharePoint list.

- Click on **Automate** > **Power Automate** > **Create a Flow**.

Step 3: Select a Workflow Template

Choose the **Start Approval When a New Item is Added** template. This template automatically routes items for approval.

Step 4: Customize the Workflow

Modify the template to suit your needs:

- **Approval Email**: Customize the message sent to approvers.

- **Conditions**: Add rules to handle rejected tasks or escalate overdue approvals.

- **Notifications**: Set up email reminders for pending approvals.

Step 5: Test the Workflow

Add a new task to your list and verify that the workflow triggers correctly. Check that notifications are sent and the task status updates as expected.

Advanced Workflow Features

Once you're comfortable with basic workflows, consider leveraging advanced features to further enhance your automation:

1. Conditional Branching

Use conditional logic to create workflows that adapt to different scenarios. For example, if a task is assigned to a specific department, route it to the appropriate manager for approval.

2. Parallel Actions

Execute multiple tasks simultaneously. For instance, notify both the project manager and the finance team when a budget request is submitted.

3. Integration with Other Tools

Connect workflows with external applications, such as Microsoft Teams or Outlook. For example, a workflow can automatically create a Teams channel for a new project listed in SharePoint.

Best Practices for Workflow Design

To ensure your workflows are efficient and reliable, follow these best practices:

1. **Keep It Simple**: Start with straightforward workflows and gradually add complexity as needed.

2. **Test Thoroughly**: Always test workflows in a staging environment before deploying them.

3. **Document Processes**: Clearly document how each workflow operates, including triggers and conditions.

4. **Monitor Performance**: Regularly review workflow performance to identify bottlenecks or errors.

5. **Update as Needed**: Continuously refine workflows to align with changing business requirements.

Common Workflow Scenarios

Here are some practical use cases for SharePoint workflows:

- **Onboarding New Employees**: Automate the distribution of onboarding materials and task assignments.

- **Expense Approvals**: Streamline the approval process for expense reports.

- **Project Management**: Automate task assignments and progress tracking.

- **Inventory Management**: Notify staff when inventory levels fall below a specified threshold.

Troubleshooting Workflow Issues

If you encounter issues with your workflows, consider these troubleshooting steps:

1. **Check Permissions**: Ensure the workflow has sufficient permissions to access the necessary list or library.

2. **Review Logs**: Use Power Automate's error logs to identify and resolve issues.

3. **Simplify Logic**: Break down complex workflows into smaller, manageable components.

Conclusion

Automating processes with workflows is a cornerstone of effective SharePoint usage. By mastering the creation and management of workflows, you can significantly enhance productivity, reduce manual errors, and empower your team to focus on high-value tasks. Take the time to experiment with different scenarios and leverage advanced features to unlock the full potential of SharePoint workflows.

4.3 Using Libraries Effectively

4.3.1 Metadata and Tags

Introduction to Metadata and Tags

Metadata and tags are foundational tools in SharePoint libraries that enhance document organization, accessibility, and usability. Metadata refers to descriptive information about your documents, such as titles, dates, authors, or custom properties. Tags, on the other hand, are labels or keywords that can be applied to files for quick identification and grouping. Together, metadata and tags transform your document library into a searchable, streamlined, and easily navigable repository.

In this section, we'll explore how metadata and tags work, why they are crucial for efficient file management, and how to implement them effectively in your SharePoint environment.

Why Use Metadata and Tags?

1. **Enhanced Search Capabilities**

   Metadata allows you to categorize files with specific attributes, making it easier for users to locate what they need. Instead of scrolling through folders, users can search by metadata fields such as project name, document type, or creation date.

2. **Improved File Organization**

   While traditional folder structures can become cumbersome as libraries grow, metadata provides a dynamic way to group and filter files. Tags further refine this process by offering flexible categorization that doesn't rely on rigid hierarchies.

3. **Supports Compliance and Governance**

   Metadata can include compliance-related fields like document retention schedules, approval statuses, or regulatory classifications. This ensures your organization adheres to industry standards and legal requirements.

4. **Streamlined Collaboration**

Tags and metadata help team members quickly identify relevant documents, reducing the time spent searching for files and improving collaboration efficiency.

Setting Up Metadata in SharePoint Libraries

1. **Adding Columns to Libraries**

   Metadata in SharePoint is implemented through columns, which represent the fields used to describe files. These columns can be added to any library:

   - **Standard Columns:** These include default fields like Title, Modified By, and Created Date.

   - **Custom Columns:** You can create columns tailored to your needs, such as "Project Name" or "Client ID."

Steps to Add Columns:

   - Navigate to your library and click on the settings gear icon.

   - Select **Library Settings > Create Column**.

   - Choose a column type (e.g., Single Line of Text, Choice, Number, Date).

   - Configure column settings, including default values, required fields, and formatting.

2. **Using Managed Metadata**

   Managed metadata is a centralized system for creating and maintaining metadata across your SharePoint environment. It allows for consistency by providing a shared vocabulary of terms.

   - **Creating a Term Set:** Go to the Term Store Management tool and define your taxonomy.

   - **Linking Metadata Columns to Term Sets:** In the library, create a new managed metadata column and associate it with a term set.

3. **Configuring Content Types**

Content types enable you to define metadata templates for specific types of documents. For example, all invoices might have predefined fields like "Invoice Number" and "Payment Due Date."

- o Set up a content type in the **Site Settings**.
- o Assign it to your library and map metadata fields.

Using Tags in SharePoint

Tags complement metadata by offering a more informal and flexible method of categorization.

1. **Creating and Applying Tags**

   Tags can be added manually by users or automatically through workflows. In SharePoint Online, tagging is often done through the document properties pane.

Steps:

- o Open a file in the library and select **Edit Properties**.
- o Add tags in the designated field.

2. **Best Practices for Tagging**

   - o **Use Consistent Terminology:** Establish guidelines for tags to avoid duplicates (e.g., "HR" vs. "Human Resources").
   - o **Combine Tags with Metadata:** Use tags for temporary or ad-hoc classification while relying on metadata for long-term organization.
   - o **Review Tags Regularly:** Periodically clean up tags to remove redundancies and ensure relevance.

Best Practices for Metadata and Tag Implementation

1. **Involve Stakeholders**

   Engage your team in defining metadata fields and tags. This ensures they meet user needs and align with organizational goals.

2. **Start Simple**

Begin with a small set of metadata fields and tags. Gradually expand as your team becomes comfortable with the system.

3. **Leverage Automation**

Use tools like Power Automate to populate metadata fields automatically based on file properties or workflows. For example, when a document is uploaded, a workflow can assign metadata based on its content.

4. **Provide Training**

Train users on how to use metadata and tags effectively. Share tutorials, conduct workshops, and create a reference guide.

Using Metadata and Tags in Advanced Scenarios

1. **Filtering and Sorting Documents**

Metadata allows users to filter and sort files in a library view. For instance, you can create a view that only shows documents tagged with "Urgent" or filter files by a specific department.

2. **Building Dynamic Views**

Dynamic views use metadata to provide tailored perspectives of your library. For example:

   - A view for "Pending Approvals" based on a status field.

   - A "Recent Uploads" view filtered by creation date.

3. **Connecting with Search**

Metadata enhances SharePoint's search functionality by indexing fields for precision. Users can perform targeted searches using keywords combined with metadata criteria.

Challenges and Solutions

1. **Metadata Overload**

Too many metadata fields can overwhelm users. Focus on essential fields and avoid unnecessary complexity.

2. **User Adoption**

   If metadata and tagging are seen as burdensome, adoption may falter. Address this by simplifying processes and demonstrating benefits.

3. **Maintenance**
   Metadata requires regular updates to remain relevant. Assign a metadata manager or administrator to oversee consistency and relevance.

Conclusion

Metadata and tags are powerful tools that elevate the functionality of SharePoint libraries. They enable better organization, improved searchability, and enhanced collaboration. By implementing these features thoughtfully and following best practices, your team can unlock the full potential of SharePoint libraries, turning them into efficient hubs of information and productivity.

4.3.2 Filtering and Sorting

Using filtering and sorting effectively within SharePoint libraries is crucial for maintaining organized and easily accessible content. These tools allow users to find specific documents quickly, streamline workflows, and enhance collaboration. This section explores the various features, techniques, and best practices for using filtering and sorting effectively in SharePoint libraries.

Understanding Filtering and Sorting in SharePoint

Filtering and sorting in SharePoint are tools designed to manage large volumes of data. Filtering narrows down the data displayed based on specific criteria, while sorting arranges the data in a particular order, such as alphabetically or numerically. Together, they make it easier to locate files, monitor changes, and analyze data trends within libraries.

- **Filtering**: Enables users to display only items that meet specific criteria, such as documents created by a particular user or files within a certain date range.

- **Sorting**: Helps in arranging data in ascending or descending order based on a selected column, such as file name, date modified, or file size.

Filtering in SharePoint Libraries

Filtering allows users to focus on a subset of files or data that meet defined parameters. SharePoint provides intuitive filtering options accessible through the library's column headers.

Basic Filtering

1. Navigate to the document library.
2. Click the filter icon next to a column header (e.g., "Name" or "Modified By").
3. Select the criteria you want to filter by, such as specific text, date ranges, or users.

Advanced Filtering with Views

For more complex filtering needs, SharePoint supports creating custom views.

- **Steps to Create a Filtered View**:
    1. Go to the library settings and select "Create View."
    2. Choose the type of view (Standard, Datasheet, Calendar, etc.).
    3. In the filter section, define the conditions. For example, "Show items where 'Modified' is greater than [Specific Date]."
    4. Save the view for future use.

Dynamic Filters
Dynamic filters adapt based on user input or current data context. For example:

- **[Me] Filter**: Displays only the files created or modified by the current user.
- **[Today] Filter**: Highlights documents modified on the current day.

Sorting in SharePoint Libraries

Sorting arranges files based on specific attributes, such as alphabetically by file name or numerically by file size. Sorting is particularly useful for libraries with hundreds or thousands of files.

Applying Basic Sorting

1. Click the column header (e.g., "Created On").

2. Select "Sort Ascending" or "Sort Descending."

3. SharePoint automatically reorganizes the library based on the selected criteria.

Multi-Level Sorting

SharePoint supports multi-level sorting for scenarios requiring more complex arrangements. For instance, you might sort files first by "Author" and then by "Date Modified."

- **Steps for Multi-Level Sorting**:

    1. Open the library settings.

    2. Configure sorting options under "Modify View."

    3. Specify multiple levels of sorting, such as primary and secondary criteria.

Combining Filtering and Sorting

The true power of SharePoint's libraries lies in combining filtering and sorting for precise data organization. For instance:

- **Example Use Case**: Filtering a library to display only documents modified by "John Doe" in the last 30 days and sorting these by "File Size" in descending order.

How to Combine:

1. Apply the filter first using the column filters.

2. Then, apply the sorting criteria on the filtered results.

Best Practices for Filtering and Sorting

To maximize the efficiency of filtering and sorting in SharePoint, consider these best practices:

1. **Use Metadata**: Metadata tags make filtering more precise. Ensure documents are tagged with relevant properties like department, status, or project name.

2. **Create Default Views**: Set up commonly used filters and sorts as default views to save time. For example, a "Recent Files" view can filter files modified in the past week and sort them by date.

3. **Leverage Filters in Workflows**: Integrate filtering into workflows to automate file organization and reduce manual effort.

4. **Avoid Overlapping Filters**: Too many filters can exclude relevant files. Use clear and specific criteria.

Advanced Features for Filtering and Sorting

SharePoint offers advanced tools and integrations to enhance filtering and sorting:

Using Column Formatting

Custom formatting can make it easier to visually differentiate data in columns. For example:

- Highlight overdue documents with red text.

- Use icons to represent different file types.

Integrating Power BI

SharePoint libraries can be integrated with Power BI for advanced filtering, sorting, and visualization. This is especially useful for analyzing large datasets or generating reports.

Custom Scripts with PowerShell

For administrators managing enterprise-level libraries, PowerShell scripts can automate complex filtering and sorting tasks. For instance, a script could generate monthly reports by filtering libraries based on specific metadata.

Troubleshooting Common Issues

Even with intuitive tools, users may encounter challenges when filtering and sorting:

- **Issue 1: Filters Not Returning Results**

    o Ensure metadata fields are correctly filled.

    o Check for permissions restricting access to certain files.

- **Issue 2: Sorting Is Incorrect**

    o Verify data types in columns. Numeric sorting may fail if numbers are stored as text.

- **Issue 3: Performance Slowdowns**

- o Large libraries with complex filters can slow down. Consider archiving old files to optimize performance.

Conclusion

Filtering and sorting are indispensable tools for managing SharePoint libraries. By mastering these features, users can boost productivity, maintain organization, and improve collaboration. Whether you're handling a small project library or a large enterprise repository, effective filtering and sorting can make navigating SharePoint a seamless experience.

CHAPTER V
Communication and Collaboration

5.1 Integrating with Microsoft Teams

SharePoint and Microsoft Teams are powerful tools that, when integrated, provide seamless collaboration, communication, and document management. This section focuses on setting up a SharePoint channel within Microsoft Teams, enabling teams to work more effectively by connecting the collaborative features of both platforms.

5.1.1 Setting Up a SharePoint Channel

Setting up a SharePoint channel in Microsoft Teams is the foundation for integrating the two platforms. This process allows team members to access SharePoint documents, resources, and tools directly within Teams, reducing the need to switch between applications and improving productivity.

Step 1: Understanding the Integration

Before diving into the setup process, it's important to understand how SharePoint and Teams work together:

- **Document Management**: Teams channels can be linked to specific SharePoint document libraries. Any file shared in Teams is stored in the associated SharePoint site.

- **Collaboration**: SharePoint pages and lists can be embedded in Teams tabs, making critical information easily accessible to team members.

- **Communication**: SharePoint news posts and updates can be integrated into Teams for improved visibility.

By combining SharePoint's robust file management with Teams' communication features, organizations create a centralized hub for collaboration.

Step 2: Linking a SharePoint Site to a Teams Channel

To begin setting up a SharePoint channel in Teams:

1. **Create or Select a Team in Microsoft Teams**

   o Open Microsoft Teams and navigate to the desired team where you want to link SharePoint.

   o Ensure that the team has an associated SharePoint site. Each team in Microsoft Teams automatically generates a corresponding SharePoint site.

2. **Go to the Desired Channel**

   o Select the specific channel within the team where you want to integrate SharePoint resources.

   o Note that each channel corresponds to a folder in the SharePoint document library.

3. **Add a SharePoint Tab**

   o In the selected channel, click the **"+" icon** in the tab bar at the top. This action opens the "Add a Tab" menu.

   o Search for and select the **"Document Library"** option.

4. **Choose the SharePoint Document Library**

   o In the setup menu, you can either choose the default document library associated with the team's SharePoint site or link to a library from another SharePoint site.

   o Use the **URL of the library** if linking to an external SharePoint site.

5. **Name and Save the Tab**

   o Assign a clear name to the tab, such as "Project Files" or "Shared Resources," to help team members identify its purpose.

   o Click **Save** to complete the setup.

Now, the selected SharePoint library will appear as a tab in the Teams channel, providing easy access to documents and files.

Step 3: Embedding SharePoint Pages and Lists

In addition to document libraries, you can embed specific SharePoint pages or lists as tabs in Teams channels:

- **Embedding a Page**:

   o Navigate to the page in SharePoint you want to embed.

   o Copy its URL and add it as a "Website" tab in Teams.

- **Embedding a List**:

   o Use the same "Add a Tab" menu to link SharePoint lists directly, enabling task tracking or data management within Teams.

Step 4: Synchronizing Permissions

Integration works best when permissions are consistent between Teams and SharePoint:

- SharePoint permissions determine who can access files in Teams.

- Always verify that team members have appropriate access levels to avoid issues.

To ensure smooth collaboration:

- Use SharePoint's permission settings to manage access.

- Regularly review permissions to align with team changes.

Step 5: Customizing Notifications

Leverage notifications to keep team members informed about SharePoint updates:

- Use **Power Automate** to create workflows that notify the Teams channel of changes in SharePoint files or lists.

- Configure alerts in SharePoint to push updates directly to Teams, ensuring no critical information is missed.

Best Practices for a Seamless Integration

1. **Organize Document Libraries**: Ensure SharePoint libraries are well-structured with clear folder names and metadata to make navigation intuitive.

2. **Train Team Members**: Provide training on how to use the integrated features effectively, including file sharing, commenting, and accessing SharePoint resources within Teams.

3. **Utilize Search Features**: Use Teams' search bar to locate SharePoint content quickly.

Common Challenges and Solutions

1. **Permissions Conflicts**:
   - Issue: Users might encounter access errors if permissions are misaligned.
   - Solution: Regularly audit permissions in both SharePoint and Teams.

2. **File Sync Issues**:
   - Issue: Changes made in SharePoint may not appear immediately in Teams.
   - Solution: Use the **"Sync" feature** in SharePoint to ensure local copies are updated.

3. **Navigation Confusion**:
   - Issue: Team members might struggle with locating files across platforms.
   - Solution: Create clear naming conventions for tabs and files to reduce confusion.

Conclusion

Setting up a SharePoint channel in Microsoft Teams unlocks powerful synergies between the two platforms, streamlining document management and fostering efficient collaboration. By following these steps, teams can harness the full potential of this integration, creating a seamless workflow environment where communication and collaboration thrive.

5.1.2 Sharing Files via Teams

One of the most powerful features of integrating SharePoint with Microsoft Teams is the ability to share files seamlessly between these two platforms. This integration allows users to collaborate more effectively, eliminate redundancies, and ensure that everyone has access to the latest version of shared files. In this section, we'll explore the key steps and best practices for sharing files via Teams, along with some advanced tips to maximize your productivity.

Understanding How SharePoint Files Work in Teams

When you create a new Team in Microsoft Teams, a SharePoint site is automatically created in the background. This SharePoint site acts as the central storage location for all files shared within the Team. Every channel within a Team corresponds to a folder in the SharePoint document library, ensuring that all files are organized and easily accessible.

This structure means that any file shared in Teams is automatically stored in SharePoint, allowing users to access files either through Teams or directly from SharePoint. Additionally, changes made to files in either platform are synchronized in real-time.

Steps to Share Files in Teams

1. Sharing Files in a Channel

- Navigate to the desired channel in Teams.

- Click on the **Files** tab at the top of the channel.

- Use the **Upload** button to add files from your local device. Alternatively, you can drag and drop files directly into the Files tab.

- Once uploaded, the file will be stored in the corresponding SharePoint folder for that channel.

2. Sharing Files in a Chat

- Open a one-on-one or group chat in Teams.

- Click on the **Attach** icon (a paperclip) in the message box.

- Choose whether to upload a file from your local device or select one from your SharePoint or OneDrive storage.

- After sending the file, it will be accessible to all participants in the chat.

3. Sharing Links to SharePoint Files

- Navigate to the file in SharePoint or Teams.

- Click on the **Share** button next to the file name.

- Configure the sharing settings, such as allowing editing or setting expiration dates for the link.

- Copy the link and paste it into a Teams message or channel post.

Best Practices for Sharing Files via Teams

1. **Maintain a Clear File Structure**

   To ensure that files are easy to find, maintain a logical folder structure in your SharePoint library. Use meaningful names for folders and files, and avoid cluttering the root directory.

2. **Set Appropriate Permissions**

   Before sharing files, verify that the correct permissions are in place. While Teams manages permissions at the channel level, you can customize SharePoint permissions for individual files or folders if needed.

3. **Encourage Version Control**

4. Teams and SharePoint automatically save previous versions of files. Educate team members on how to access version history to review changes or revert to an earlier version if necessary.

5. **Avoid Duplication**

   Instead of downloading and re-uploading files, use links to SharePoint files. This ensures everyone is working on the same document, reducing the risk of duplication or outdated versions.

6. **Leverage Metadata**

   Use metadata in SharePoint to categorize files with tags or labels. This can make it easier to filter and search for files in Teams, especially in large projects.

Collaborative Features in Teams for File Sharing

Real-Time Co-Authoring

When a file is shared in Teams, users can co-author the document using Microsoft Office Online. Multiple users can edit the document simultaneously, with changes synced in real-time. This feature eliminates the need to send files back and forth via email.

Comments and Mentions

Within shared files, team members can leave comments or use @mentions to direct feedback to specific individuals. This fosters collaboration and ensures that important feedback is not overlooked.

Tabs for Quick Access

For frequently used files, consider adding them as a tab in the channel. This makes the file easily accessible to all members without needing to navigate the Files tab each time.

Advanced Tips for File Sharing in Teams

1. Automate File Management with Power Automate

Integrate Power Automate to automate repetitive tasks related to file sharing. For instance, you can create a workflow to notify team members when a new file is uploaded or move files to a specific folder based on naming conventions.

2. Set Up Alerts for Important Files

In SharePoint, set up alerts for critical files to receive email notifications when changes are made. This ensures that team members stay informed about updates.

3. Use Sensitivity Labels

To protect sensitive information, apply sensitivity labels to files in SharePoint. These labels ensure that only authorized users can access or edit the files, adding an extra layer of security.

4. Sync Files Locally

If you frequently work offline, sync SharePoint files to your local device using OneDrive. This allows you to access and edit files offline, with changes synced back to SharePoint when you reconnect.

Common Challenges and Solutions

Challenge 1: Files Not Accessible to All Team Members

- **Solution:** Check the permissions settings in SharePoint. Ensure that all team members have the required access level.

Challenge 2: Difficulty Finding Shared Files

- **Solution:** Use the search bar in the Files tab or apply filters based on file type, date, or metadata.

Challenge 3: File Conflicts During Collaboration

- **Solution:** Encourage real-time co-authoring and educate team members on how to resolve conflicts using version history.

Conclusion

Sharing files via Teams is a straightforward yet powerful feature that enhances collaboration and productivity. By understanding the underlying integration with SharePoint, users can make the most of both platforms, ensuring efficient and secure file sharing. Whether you're working on a small project or managing a large team, following the best practices and tips outlined in this section will help you streamline your workflows and foster a more collaborative environment.

5.2 SharePoint News Features

5.2.1 Publishing News Posts

SharePoint News is a powerful tool for keeping your team informed, engaged, and aligned. By creating and publishing news posts, you can share updates, announcements, and other important information across your organization in a centralized, professional, and visually appealing manner. This section will guide you through the process of creating effective news posts, customizing them to fit your needs, and ensuring they reach the right audience.

What Are News Posts in SharePoint?

News posts in SharePoint function as a communication tool designed to keep everyone in your organization on the same page. Unlike standard posts in discussion boards or basic email updates, SharePoint news posts allow for rich formatting, multimedia integration, and centralized accessibility. They can include images, links, videos, and even embedded files, making them a versatile option for delivering content that stands out.

Benefits of Using News Posts

- **Centralized Communication**: SharePoint News ensures that important updates are not lost in email chains or chat messages.

- **Audience Targeting**: News posts can be targeted to specific groups, ensuring that the right people receive relevant information.

- **Professional Presentation**: With templates and formatting tools, news posts look polished and professional.

- **Engagement Metrics**: Built-in analytics let you track who has read the news and gauge its impact.

Creating a News Post

Publishing a SharePoint news post is a straightforward process, but there are multiple steps to ensure it is impactful and reaches the intended audience.

Step 1: Navigate to Your Site's News Section

1. Go to your SharePoint team or communication site.

2. Locate the **News** section, typically found on the homepage or under a dedicated tab.

Step 2: Select "Add News Post"

1. Click the **Add** button or the **+** sign within the News section.

2. Choose **News Post** from the menu. Alternatively, you can select **News Link** to highlight external content.

Step 3: Choose a Template

SharePoint provides several templates designed for different types of news, such as announcements, event updates, and progress reports. Select a template that best fits your content.

- **Blank Template**: For fully custom layouts.

- **Basic Text Template**: Ideal for text-heavy updates.

- **Visual Template**: Best for posts requiring images or videos.

Step 4: Add Your Content

Use the editor to craft your post:

- **Title**: Write a clear and engaging headline.

- **Body Text**: Use concise paragraphs with headings for clarity.

- **Images and Videos**: Insert visuals to enhance engagement.

- **Links and Attachments**: Add hyperlinks or attach documents for additional resources.

Step 5: Customize the Layout

- Drag and drop web parts to rearrange the layout.

- Use **Sections** to divide content visually, such as adding columns for side-by-side comparisons.

Best Practices for News Posts

To maximize the impact of your news post, keep the following tips in mind:

- **Keep It Relevant**: Focus on content that is timely and important for your audience.

- **Use Visuals Effectively**: High-quality images and videos grab attention and reinforce your message.

- **Write for Your Audience**: Tailor the tone and complexity of your writing to your readers.

- **Include a Call to Action**: If your post is intended to prompt action, make this clear with a button or highlighted text.

Publishing Your News Post

Once your post is ready:

1. Click **Publish** in the top-right corner of the editor.

2. Review the settings for audience targeting. If necessary, adjust permissions to ensure the intended readers can view the content.

3. Add tags or metadata to improve discoverability.

Scheduling News Posts

In some cases, you may want to schedule a news post for future publication. This feature allows you to prepare posts in advance while maintaining a consistent communication cadence.

1. Click the drop-down menu next to the **Publish** button.

2. Select **Schedule for Later** and choose your desired date and time.

3. Save the settings and ensure all content is finalized before the scheduled time.

Tracking Engagement

After publishing a news post, it's essential to monitor its performance. SharePoint provides built-in analytics tools that allow you to track:

- **Page Views**: The number of people who viewed the post.

- **Engagement Metrics**: Actions taken after reading, such as comments or clicks on links.

- **Audience Reach**: Demographics of readers, such as department or team.

These insights can help you refine future posts and ensure they resonate with your audience.

Common Challenges and Solutions

- **Low Engagement**: Experiment with more eye-catching visuals or concise messaging.

- **Permission Issues**: Double-check access settings before publishing.

- **Formatting Problems**: Use the preview feature to identify and fix layout inconsistencies.

By mastering the art of publishing news posts in SharePoint, you can transform how your team communicates and collaborates, fostering a more informed and engaged workplace. Up next, learn how to use news highlights to amplify your most important updates.

5.2.2 Highlighting Important Updates

SharePoint's ability to highlight important updates through its News feature is a cornerstone for effective communication within an organization. This functionality enables teams to keep everyone informed, streamline decision-making, and foster a collaborative environment. In this section, we will explore the steps to create visually compelling updates, best practices for targeting content to the right audience, and tips for maintaining engagement.

Crafting Visually Engaging Updates

Highlighting important updates begins with creating content that captures attention. SharePoint News allows you to incorporate rich media, structured layouts, and compelling text to communicate effectively. Here's how you can create updates that stand out:

1. Use Visual Hierarchy

- **Titles and Headers:** Use large, bold titles to immediately convey the subject of your update. Subheaders can break content into digestible sections.

- **Images and Videos:** Incorporate high-quality visuals to support your message. A compelling image or a short video clip can help capture attention more effectively than plain text.

2. Leverage Prebuilt Templates

SharePoint offers templates specifically designed for News posts. Use these templates to ensure a professional and visually appealing structure. Customize them to reflect the tone and branding of your organization.

3. Embed Interactive Content

Embed charts, graphs, or live dashboards into your updates to provide real-time data insights. These interactive elements not only make your content more engaging but also provide value to the audience.

Targeting Updates to the Right Audience

One of SharePoint's standout features is its ability to target News updates to specific groups or individuals. This ensures that the right people see the information they need, reducing clutter for others.

1. Using Targeted Audience Features

- Enable **audience targeting** in your SharePoint settings. This allows you to specify user groups that will see the update on their News feed.

- Group audiences based on factors like departments, roles, or geographic location to tailor updates effectively.

2. Segmenting Content by Relevance

Not all updates are relevant to every employee. Segment your content by creating distinct News categories (e.g., "HR Updates," "IT Announcements," "Project Highlights") to make it easy for users to find updates relevant to them.

3. Incorporating Personalized Feeds

Enable personalized News feeds where users only see content tagged for their audience group. This reduces information overload and enhances the user experience.

Formatting Best Practices for Highlighting Updates

The presentation of an update significantly influences how well it is received. Follow these formatting best practices to maximize impact:

1. Keep It Concise

While SharePoint allows for detailed posts, aim to keep your content concise. Focus on the most critical points and use links or attachments for additional information.

2. Use Call-to-Action Buttons

Incorporate buttons like "Read More," "Register Now," or "Explore Details" to guide users toward taking the next step. These actions can link to event registrations, detailed reports, or additional resources.

3. Optimize for Mobile Devices

With many employees accessing updates on mobile devices, ensure that your News posts are mobile-friendly. Test layouts and visuals for responsiveness.

Driving Engagement with Highlighted Updates

Creating a great update is only half the battle; you also need to ensure that employees engage with the content. Here are strategies to achieve this:

1. Promoting News Updates

- Pin critical updates to the top of the News feed or homepage to ensure visibility.

- Use email notifications to alert employees to high-priority announcements.

2. Encouraging Interactions

- Enable comments and likes on News posts to foster discussions and feedback.

- Encourage team leaders or managers to engage with posts by commenting or sharing them.

3. Using Analytics to Improve Engagement

SharePoint Analytics provides insights into how users interact with your News updates. Monitor metrics like views, likes, and shares to refine your approach.

Case Study: Highlighting Updates in Action

Scenario: A manufacturing company uses SharePoint to announce a major system upgrade across all its facilities.

Approach:

1. **Targeted Content:** The IT department targets News updates to specific user groups (e.g., factory workers, office staff) with tailored messages for each group.

2. **Visual Appeal:** Posts include a short video walkthrough of the new system and a downloadable user guide.

3. **Interactive Elements:** A FAQ section with collapsible panels is embedded directly in the News post.

4. **Follow-Up Engagement:** Notifications are sent to remind employees to read the update, and a survey link is included to gather feedback on the new system.

Outcome: The post garners high engagement, with 85% of employees accessing the content within 48 hours. The feedback survey provides actionable insights for the IT team.

Maintaining a Consistent Update Strategy

To maximize the benefits of SharePoint News, it's important to maintain consistency in your update strategy. Develop a content calendar for major announcements, team highlights, and industry news. Regular updates foster a sense of community and keep employees informed.

1. Establish a Posting Schedule

Regular updates, such as weekly highlights or monthly announcements, help employees know when to expect new content.

2. Rotate Contributors

Encourage different departments to contribute News posts. This diversifies the content and ensures a broader range of updates.

3. Review and Revise

Periodically review the effectiveness of your News updates. Use analytics to identify areas for improvement and adjust your strategy accordingly.

Highlighting important updates through SharePoint's News features is an excellent way to ensure your organization stays informed and engaged. By leveraging the platform's robust tools for targeting, formatting, and promoting content, you can create updates that resonate with your audience and drive meaningful collaboration.

5.3 Using Discussion Boards

5.3.1 Starting Conversations

Discussion boards in SharePoint serve as a dynamic platform for team communication, idea sharing, and problem-solving. They allow teams to engage in structured discussions, making it easier to manage and reference conversations over time. This section delves into how to effectively start conversations in a SharePoint discussion board to foster collaboration and engagement.

Understanding the Purpose of Discussion Boards

Before starting a conversation, it's essential to recognize the purpose of discussion boards. Unlike informal chats or emails, discussion boards are designed for:

- **Organized Communication:** Conversations are categorized into threads, making it easier to track topics and responses.

- **Collaboration:** They encourage team participation and input, promoting knowledge sharing.

- **Record-Keeping:** Discussion boards serve as a repository of ideas, allowing users to revisit important discussions.

With this in mind, users can leverage discussion boards as a strategic tool for productive team collaboration.

Steps to Start a Conversation

1. **Access the Discussion Board**

   o Navigate to your SharePoint site and locate the discussion board.

   o If a discussion board hasn't been created, follow these steps:

      1. Go to the **Site Contents** section of your SharePoint site.

      2. Select **New App** and choose **Discussion Board** from the app list.

   3. Name the discussion board and configure its settings.

2. **Click 'New Discussion'**

   o   Open the discussion board and click on the **New Discussion** button. This action initiates the process of starting a conversation thread.

3. **Enter a Clear and Concise Title**

   o   Provide a descriptive title that summarizes the topic.

   o   Examples:

      ▪   "Best Practices for Project Management"

      ▪   "Feedback on New Marketing Campaign"

      ▪   "Suggestions for Team Outing Locations"

A clear title helps team members quickly identify the subject and decide if they want to participate.

4. **Compose the Initial Post**

   o   Write a detailed message that provides context and sets the tone for the discussion.

   o   Consider the following elements:

      ▪   **Background Information:** Explain why the topic is important.

      ▪   **Key Questions:** Include specific questions to guide the discussion.

      ▪   **Attachments or Links:** Share relevant documents, links, or resources.

Example:

Title: Feedback on New Marketing Campaign

Message:
Hi Team,

We recently launched our new campaign, and I'd like to gather your feedback. Please share your thoughts on the visuals, messaging, and overall impact. Attached are the campaign details and analytics from the first week. Looking forward to hearing your input!

5. **Use Formatting Tools**

   o SharePoint discussion boards include basic formatting tools. Use these to make your post more readable:

      ▪ **Bold** or *italicize* text for emphasis.

      ▪ Add bullet points or numbered lists for clarity.

      ▪ Use hyperlinks to direct users to external resources.

Best Practices for Starting Conversations

1. **Be Specific**
   Avoid vague topics like "Important Update" or "Thoughts Needed." Instead, provide specific titles and messages to focus the discussion.

2. **Set Expectations**
   Clearly state what you expect from participants, such as providing suggestions, voting on ideas, or sharing experiences.

3. **Encourage Participation**

   o Use inclusive language like "I'd love to hear everyone's thoughts on this" or "Your input will help us improve."

   o Tag relevant team members by name to ensure they see the discussion.

4. **Keep It Professional**
   While discussion boards are less formal than emails, maintain a professional tone to ensure clarity and respect.

Examples of Effective Conversation Starters

- **Example 1: Brainstorming Ideas**

Title: Ideas for Upcoming Team Workshop

Message:
Hi Everyone,

We're planning a team workshop next month, and I'd like your input on the topics we should   cover.
Please share your suggestions for activities, guest speakers, or themes. Let's make this event engaging and valuable!

- **Example 2: Addressing Challenges**

Title: Resolving Client Onboarding Issues

Message:
Hi Team,

Recently, we've encountered delays in the client onboarding process. I'd like to discuss the   challenges   and   brainstorm   solutions.
Please share your experiences and any ideas for streamlining the workflow.

Encouraging Engagement

Once the initial conversation is posted, it's essential to foster engagement:

- **Acknowledge Responses:** Thank team members for their contributions and highlight valuable insights.

- **Follow Up:** If there's limited participation, prompt users with specific questions or share additional context.

- **Summarize Discussions:** Periodically summarize key points in the thread to keep the conversation organized.

Conclusion

Starting conversations in SharePoint discussion boards is a straightforward yet impactful way to drive team collaboration. By crafting clear, engaging, and purposeful posts, you can create a productive environment for exchanging ideas and solving problems. In the next section, we'll explore strategies for moderating discussions to ensure they remain focused and valuable.

5.3.2 Moderating Discussions

Moderating discussions on SharePoint discussion boards is crucial to ensure that conversations remain productive, relevant, and respectful. As a moderator, your role extends beyond managing content—it also involves fostering engagement, addressing issues proactively, and maintaining a collaborative environment. This section outlines key strategies, tools, and best practices for effective discussion moderation.

The Role of a Discussion Moderator

Moderators act as facilitators in SharePoint discussion boards, ensuring that the platform is a safe and effective space for collaboration. The responsibilities include:

- **Monitoring Content:** Ensuring posts adhere to company policies and community guidelines.

- **Encouraging Participation:** Creating an inviting atmosphere that motivates users to contribute.

- **Resolving Conflicts:** Addressing disputes or inappropriate behavior diplomatically.

- **Curating Information:** Highlighting valuable contributions and summarizing key points.

By fulfilling these roles, moderators help transform discussion boards into powerful tools for collaboration and innovation.

Key Features for Moderating Discussions

SharePoint offers a range of tools and features that support moderation. Familiarity with these functionalities can enhance your efficiency as a moderator.

1. **Permissions Management**
   - Set specific permissions for users to post, edit, or delete their contributions.

- o Assign moderator privileges to trusted team members to share the responsibility.

2. **Content Filtering**

   - o Use automated filters to detect and flag inappropriate language or spam.

   - o Create rules to prevent off-topic posts by enforcing structured discussion categories.

3. **Notifications and Alerts**

   - o Enable alerts to stay updated on new posts and comments.

   - o Customize notifications for critical discussions or flagged content.

4. **Moderation Queue**

   - o Review and approve posts before they appear on the board to maintain quality control.

   - o Provide feedback to users if their content requires revisions.

5. **Search and Tagging Features**

   - o Leverage tagging to categorize discussions for easier navigation.

   - o Use search filters to locate specific threads or monitor recurring issues.

Best Practices for Effective Moderation

1. **Establish Clear Guidelines**

   - o Define the purpose and scope of the discussion board.

   - o Share guidelines on expected behavior, posting etiquette, and acceptable content.

   - o Pin the guidelines at the top of the board for easy access.

2. **Promote Constructive Interactions**

   - o Encourage users to share diverse perspectives while respecting differing opinions.

- o Acknowledge valuable contributions by liking or replying to posts.

- o Highlight well-crafted posts or solutions in a "Featured Discussions" section.

3. **Address Conflicts Promptly**

   - o Intervene early in heated discussions to prevent escalation.

   - o Privately communicate with users involved in conflicts to mediate and resolve issues.

   - o Remove inflammatory or inappropriate content as needed, documenting your actions for transparency.

4. **Monitor Participation Levels**

   - o Identify inactive users and encourage them to join discussions.

   - o Offer incentives, such as recognition or rewards, for active contributors.

5. **Encourage Feedback**

   - o Regularly ask users for suggestions to improve the board's functionality.

   - o Implement feasible changes and communicate updates to the community.

Common Challenges in Moderating SharePoint Discussions

While moderating discussions can be rewarding, it also comes with challenges. Being aware of these obstacles and preparing strategies to address them can make your role as a moderator more manageable.

1. **Low Engagement**

   - o **Solution:** Post open-ended questions or initiate discussions on trending topics to spark interest. Share case studies, relevant news, or thought-provoking content to draw users in.

2. **Irrelevant or Spam Content**

   - o **Solution:** Utilize automated content filters and review flagged posts regularly. Educate users on the importance of staying on-topic.

3. **Conflict Resolution**

   o **Solution:** Apply conflict-resolution techniques, such as active listening and neutral mediation. If necessary, escalate issues to higher authorities for resolution.

4. **Overwhelming Volume of Posts**

   o **Solution:** Divide the board into categories and assign multiple moderators to manage specific sections. Use SharePoint's analytics to identify high-traffic areas requiring additional attention.

Leveraging Analytics for Better Moderation

SharePoint provides analytics tools to help moderators monitor user activity and identify trends. Utilize these insights to improve moderation strategies:

- **User Engagement Metrics:** Track the number of posts, comments, and active participants.

- **Sentiment Analysis:** Identify posts with positive or negative sentiment to gauge the board's atmosphere.

- **Topic Popularity:** Determine which discussion topics generate the most interest and focus on promoting similar content.

Fostering a Collaborative Community

Moderation is not just about managing content—it's about building a thriving community. Here are some tips to foster collaboration:

- **Host Regular Events:** Schedule Q&A sessions, expert-led discussions, or themed weeks to maintain engagement.

- **Recognize Contributors:** Highlight top contributors through badges, mentions, or a leaderboard.

- **Encourage Peer Moderation:** Empower users to flag inappropriate content and suggest improvements.

By creating a supportive and engaging environment, discussion boards can become invaluable resources for knowledge sharing and team collaboration.

Moderating SharePoint discussion boards effectively requires a combination of technical skills, interpersonal expertise, and a proactive mindset. By implementing these strategies, you can ensure your discussion board remains a vibrant and collaborative space that meets your organization's needs.

CHAPTER VI
Customizing Your SharePoint Experience

6.1 Using Web Parts

Web Parts are one of the most powerful and flexible features in SharePoint, enabling users to add dynamic content and interactive elements to their pages. They act as building blocks, allowing you to tailor SharePoint pages to suit your team's needs and organizational goals. In this section, we'll explore how to effectively use Web Parts, starting with adding them to pages.

6.1.1 Adding Web Parts to Pages

Adding Web Parts to SharePoint pages is a straightforward process, but understanding how and where to place them is critical to designing an efficient and visually appealing site. This subsection will guide you through the steps to add Web Parts to pages, discuss best practices, and highlight common use cases.

Understanding the Role of Web Parts

Web Parts serve as modular components that provide functionality such as displaying data, integrating third-party tools, or facilitating collaboration. For instance, you can use a Document Library Web Part to showcase important files, a News Web Part to share updates, or a Quick Links Web Part to direct users to frequently accessed resources.

Step-by-Step Guide to Adding Web Parts

Follow these steps to add Web Parts to your SharePoint pages:

1. **Navigate to the Page**

   Open the SharePoint site and navigate to the page where you want to add a Web Part. If you do not have an existing page, create one by selecting **New Page** from the Site Contents menu.

2. **Enter Edit Mode**
   Click on the **Edit** button in the top-right corner of the page. This action unlocks the page layout and allows you to add, move, or customize Web Parts.

3. **Select a Section Layout**

   Before adding a Web Part, decide on the section layout. SharePoint offers various layout options, such as single-column, two-column, or three-column sections. To add a section:

   o   Click the **+** icon on the page.

   o   Select the desired section layout.

4. **Add a Web Part**

   o   In the section you've created, click the **+** button within the desired column or area.

   o   A panel will appear on the right side, showcasing all available Web Parts.

   o   Scroll through the list or use the search bar to find the Web Part you need.

5. **Configure the Web Part**

   Once added, click on the Web Part to open its settings panel. This panel allows you to customize the Web Part's content, appearance, and behavior.

Best Practices for Adding Web Parts

To make the most of Web Parts, keep the following best practices in mind:

- **Prioritize Functionality**: Choose Web Parts that add value to your page's purpose. For example, a Calendar Web Part is ideal for team schedules, while a News Web Part suits announcements.

- **Maintain Visual Consistency**: Use Web Parts that align with your site's theme and branding. Customize fonts, colors, and layouts to ensure a cohesive design.

- **Test User Experience**: Preview the page to ensure Web Parts function as intended and provide an intuitive experience for users.

Commonly Used Web Parts

SharePoint offers a variety of Web Parts to cater to diverse needs. Here are some of the most popular ones and their use cases:

1. **Document Library Web Part**

   Displays files stored in a document library, allowing users to access, upload, or manage documents directly from the page.

2. **Quick Links Web Part**

   Provides a customizable set of links to frequently used sites, documents, or tools. Ideal for enhancing navigation.

3. **News Web Part**

   Shares recent updates, announcements, or blog posts with your audience.

4. **Image Web Part**

   Displays images to enhance the visual appeal of your page. Useful for banners, team photos, or infographics.

5. **Embed Web Part**

   Integrates external content such as YouTube videos or Google Maps directly into your SharePoint page.

Advanced Configurations

Some Web Parts, such as Lists or Power BI Reports, require additional setup for full functionality. For example:

- **Lists Web Part**: Requires an existing SharePoint list with defined columns and data.

- **Power BI Web Part**: Needs a valid Power BI report link and appropriate permissions.

Troubleshooting Common Issues

While adding Web Parts is generally smooth, you may encounter the following challenges:

- **Web Part Not Displaying Correctly**: Ensure the Web Part is configured properly and that the necessary data sources are connected.

- **Permissions Issues**: Users may need appropriate permissions to view or interact with certain Web Parts.

- **Slow Load Times**: Optimize the page by minimizing the number of Web Parts or compressing large images.

Conclusion

Adding Web Parts to your SharePoint pages is a powerful way to enhance functionality and improve user engagement. By following the steps outlined above and adhering to best practices, you can design pages that meet your organization's needs effectively.

In the next section, we will explore how to customize Web Part settings to further tailor their functionality and appearance to your unique requirements.

6.1.2 Customizing Web Part Settings

Web parts are one of the most powerful features of SharePoint, enabling users to enhance their sites with dynamic content, tools, and functionality. Once you've added a web part to a page, the next step is tailoring it to meet your specific needs. Customizing web part settings not only ensures that the web part fits seamlessly into your site but also enhances user engagement and usability.

In this section, we'll explore the key steps and best practices for customizing web part settings, providing detailed guidance on achieving optimal results.

Understanding Web Part Settings

Each web part in SharePoint comes with a unique set of configurable settings. These settings allow you to:

- **Adjust the layout**: Define how the web part is displayed on the page.

- **Filter and sort content**: Control the type of content shown within the web part.

- **Apply audience targeting**: Ensure that specific users or groups see tailored content.

- **Modify appearance**: Customize colors, fonts, and alignment to align with your site's design.

While the options may vary depending on the type of web part you're using (e.g., document library, news feed, or image gallery), the process of customization generally follows a similar flow.

Steps to Customize Web Part Settings

Step 1: Open the Web Part Settings Panel

1. **Enter Edit Mode**: Navigate to the page containing the web part you want to customize and click the gear icon in the top right corner. Select **Edit Page** from the dropdown menu.

2. **Access Settings**: Hover over the web part to reveal its toolbar. Click the pencil icon (**Edit Web Part**) to open the settings panel on the right side of the screen.

Step 2: Configure Display Settings

The display settings define how the web part appears on the page. Key options include:

- **Width and height**: Adjust these to ensure the web part fits neatly without overwhelming the page.

- **Alignment**: Align the web part to the left, center, or right.

- **Section layout**: Some web parts allow adjustments to the section it resides in, such as splitting the section into columns or changing its background color.

Step 3: Adjust Content Filters and Sorting

For web parts that display lists, libraries, or dynamic content (e.g., recent documents, upcoming events), filters and sorting options are critical:

- **Apply filters**: Use criteria like file type, author, or created date to control what content appears. For example, in a document library web part, you might filter by file type to only display PDFs.

- **Sort content**: Choose whether items are displayed alphabetically, by date, or by custom order.

Step 4: Enable Audience Targeting

Audience targeting is a powerful feature that allows you to tailor the content of a web part to specific groups or individuals.

- **Activate Targeting**: In the settings panel, locate the audience targeting toggle and enable it.

- **Assign Groups**: Add user groups or individuals who should see the content. This is especially useful for displaying personalized dashboards or team-specific announcements.

Step 5: Customize the Appearance

The appearance options let you align the web part's style with your site's branding.

- **Themes**: Select a pre-defined theme or create a custom color palette.

- **Fonts and typography**: Adjust the text size, style, and color to make the content more readable.

- **Borders and spacing**: Add or remove borders and fine-tune padding for a polished look.

Advanced Customization Techniques

Using Dynamic Data Sources

Some web parts, such as the **Highlighted Content** or **List** web parts, allow dynamic connections to data sources. For example:

- **Connect to a list or library**: Display specific items from a SharePoint list or library.

- **Use search queries**: Pull data based on keywords or metadata filters, offering a dynamic user experience.

Incorporating Conditional Formatting

Conditional formatting enables you to visually emphasize specific data in web parts. For instance:

- Highlight overdue tasks in red within a task list.

- Display high-priority news posts in bold or with an icon.

To enable conditional formatting, access the settings panel and look for formatting rules under the **Conditional Formatting** section.

Best Practices for Customizing Web Parts

1. **Start Simple**: Avoid overloading web parts with excessive content or styling. Focus on clarity and relevance.

2. **Test Across Devices**: Ensure your customizations look good on both desktop and mobile devices. Use the SharePoint mobile app or resize your browser window to preview.

3. **Use Consistent Themes**: Maintain uniformity in colors and fonts across all web parts to ensure a cohesive site design.

4. **Engage Your Audience**: Take advantage of audience targeting to make your content relevant for different user groups.

Troubleshooting Customization Issues

Despite SharePoint's user-friendly interface, you might encounter challenges when customizing web parts:

- **Settings Not Saving**: Ensure you click **Publish** or **Save as Draft** after making changes.

- **Limited Options Available**: Check if you have the necessary permissions to modify web parts. Site members may need additional access rights.

- **Broken Formatting**: Revisit your customizations and reset settings if needed. Sometimes, complex formatting rules can conflict.

Real-World Example: Customizing a News Web Part

Imagine you're managing a team site and want the **News Web Part** to show only updates relevant to project deadlines:

1. **Add the News Web Part**: Place it in a prominent section of the homepage.

2. **Filter by Metadata**: Use tags like "Project Deadlines" or "Urgent Updates" to filter content.

3. **Enable Audience Targeting**: Ensure only team members can see these posts.

4. **Apply Conditional Formatting**: Highlight posts tagged as "High Priority" in red.

The result? A highly tailored and functional web part that keeps your team informed and focused.

By mastering the art of customizing web part settings, you can transform any SharePoint site into an engaging, efficient, and visually appealing workspace. Whether you're building dashboards, managing documents, or sharing news, these tools empower you to make the most of SharePoint's capabilities.

6.2 Personalizing Themes and Layouts

6.2.1 Changing Site Themes

Changing a SharePoint site's theme is one of the easiest and most effective ways to create a visually appealing and brand-consistent workspace. Themes define the color palette, font styles, and overall design aesthetic of your site, ensuring a cohesive look and feel. In this section, we will explore the importance of themes, the steps to apply and customize them, and best practices for selecting the right theme for your organization.

Understanding SharePoint Themes

A theme in SharePoint acts as a visual foundation for your site. It helps in:

- **Branding:** Aligning the site's appearance with your organization's corporate identity.

- **User Experience:** Enhancing navigation and interaction through consistent design elements.

- **Readability:** Ensuring text, background colors, and other UI components are easy to distinguish and use.

SharePoint provides several built-in themes that cater to different needs, ranging from minimalistic styles to vibrant color palettes. Additionally, administrators can create custom themes to meet specific branding requirements.

Steps to Change a Site Theme

Here is a step-by-step guide to changing a SharePoint site theme:

1. Accessing the Theme Settings

1. Navigate to your SharePoint site.

2. Click on the **Settings Gear Icon** in the upper-right corner of the screen.

3. From the dropdown menu, select **Change the Look**.

4. In the "Change the Look" panel, choose **Themes** to access the theme options.

2. Exploring Built-In Themes

SharePoint offers a variety of default themes, each optimized for usability and aesthetics.

- Preview each theme by clicking on it. The site updates in real time to show how the selected theme will look.

- If you like a theme, click **Save** to apply it permanently.

3. Customizing the Selected Theme

If the default themes don't fully align with your preferences, SharePoint allows minor customizations. For example:

- **Changing Colors:** Select from predefined color palettes or define your custom hex values.

- **Updating Fonts:** Adjust the font styles for headings and body text to suit your brand's identity.

4. Applying the Theme

Once you are satisfied with the preview, save the changes to apply the theme across your site. The changes will reflect instantly for all users who access the site.

Creating Custom Themes for Branding

While the built-in themes are sufficient for general use, organizations often need custom themes to meet branding requirements. Custom themes are created using JSON files and can be deployed by administrators.

Steps to Create a Custom Theme

1. **Draft a JSON File:**

2. Use SharePoint's theme generator tool to design a theme. This tool provides an intuitive interface for selecting colors and other parameters. The result is a JSON file.

3. **Upload the Theme to SharePoint:**

   o Access the **SharePoint Admin Center**.

   o Go to **Themes** under the admin settings.

   o Upload your JSON file and name the theme appropriately.

4. **Apply the Custom Theme:**

   After uploading, the custom theme will appear alongside the default themes in the "Change the Look" panel, making it easy for site owners to apply.

Best Practices for Selecting a Theme

Choosing the right theme can significantly impact user satisfaction and productivity. Here are some tips:

1. Focus on Accessibility

Ensure the theme provides enough contrast between text and background. This is critical for readability, especially for users with visual impairments.

2. Maintain Consistency

Use the same theme across multiple SharePoint sites in your organization to create a unified user experience.

3. Reflect Corporate Branding

Include corporate colors, logos, and font styles in the theme to reinforce brand identity.

4. Test Before Deployment

Always preview themes on different devices and browsers to ensure compatibility and usability.

Troubleshooting Theme Issues

Occasionally, users may encounter issues when changing or applying themes. Here's how to resolve common problems:

Issue 1: Theme Not Applying Properly

- **Cause:** Permissions might be restricted.
- **Solution:** Ensure the user has site owner or admin privileges.

Issue 2: Custom Theme Not Visible

- **Cause:** The JSON file may not have been uploaded correctly.
- **Solution:** Recheck the upload process and ensure the file follows SharePoint's guidelines.

Issue 3: Accessibility Concerns

- **Cause:** Inadequate color contrast.
- **Solution:** Use SharePoint's accessibility checker to identify and resolve issues.

Enhancing User Engagement with Themes

A well-designed theme does more than beautify a site; it can foster engagement and collaboration. Bright, inviting designs can make users more likely to interact with the site, while clean, professional themes can establish trust and credibility.

Encourage feedback from your team after applying a new theme. Their insights can help in fine-tuning the design for an even better user experience.

By mastering themes, you take the first step in creating a SharePoint environment that is not only functional but also inspiring. Continue to explore the customization options in the next section, where we discuss **Adjusting Navigation Menus** to enhance usability further.

6.2.2 Adjusting Navigation Menus

Navigation menus are the cornerstone of a well-structured SharePoint site, guiding users effortlessly through the content and tools they need. An intuitive, customized menu not only enhances usability but also ensures that team members can quickly locate critical resources, improving productivity. In this section, we'll explore how to adjust navigation menus to better suit the needs of your organization.

Understanding SharePoint Navigation

SharePoint offers two primary types of navigation:

1. **Top Navigation Bar**: Typically displayed at the top of your SharePoint site, this menu is ideal for linking to major sections or pages.

2. **Quick Launch (Left Navigation)**: Positioned on the left side of the page, this menu is more detailed and often used for navigating within a site.

Both types of navigation can be customized to include links to pages, document libraries, external sites, or any resources users frequently access.

Benefits of Customizing Navigation

Customizing navigation menus provides several advantages:

- **Improved User Experience**: Users can quickly find what they need without sifting through unrelated content.

- **Reflects Organizational Structure**: Menus can mimic your organization's hierarchy, making it intuitive for teams.

- **Enhances Collaboration**: Clear navigation fosters better collaboration by directing users to shared resources and tools.

- **Reduces Cognitive Load**: Well-structured menus minimize confusion and help users focus on their tasks.

Customizing the Quick Launch Menu

The Quick Launch menu is highly versatile and can be tailored to meet specific site requirements. Follow these steps to adjust it:

1. **Access the Site Settings**:

    o Navigate to your SharePoint site and click on the gear icon in the top-right corner.

    o Select **Site Settings** from the dropdown menu.

2. **Edit the Quick Launch**:

    o Under the **Look and Feel** section, click **Navigation**.

    o In the Quick Launch area, you'll see options to add, edit, or reorder links.

3. **Add a Link**:

    o Click **Add Link**.

    o Enter the URL of the page, document library, or external site you want to include.

    o Provide a name for the link, ensuring it's clear and descriptive.

4. **Reorder Links**:

    o Drag and drop links to arrange them in the desired order.

    o Group related links under logical headers for better organization.

5. **Remove Links**:

    o Click the **Edit** icon next to a link and select **Delete** to remove it from the menu.

Customizing the Top Navigation Bar

The Top Navigation Bar offers a broader perspective, connecting users to high-level sections or related sites. Here's how to adjust it:

1. **Enable Structural Navigation** (if necessary):

   o   By default, some sites use **Managed Navigation** based on metadata. Switch to **Structural Navigation** for manual control by accessing **Navigation Settings** in **Site Settings**.

2. **Add Links to the Top Navigation Bar**:

   o   In the **Global Navigation** section, click **Add Link**.

   o   Provide a descriptive title and paste the URL of the destination.

3. **Organize Menu Items**:

   o   Use submenus to group related links under dropdown headers.

   o   Click **Edit** next to a menu item, then drag it under another link to create a hierarchy.

4. **Link to External Sites**:

   o   SharePoint allows you to add external links, which can be useful for directing users to tools like Google Drive, CRM systems, or partner websites.

Tips for Effective Navigation Design

1. **Keep It Simple**:

   Avoid overloading menus with too many options. Limit the number of links and group related items logically.

2. **Use Descriptive Labels**:

   Choose names that clearly convey the purpose of each link. For example, instead of "Docs," use "Project Documents."

3. **Test Your Menu**:

Ask team members to navigate the site and gather feedback. Adjust the menu structure based on their suggestions.

4. **Review Regularly**:

As your organization evolves, update the menu to reflect changes in workflows, team priorities, or frequently accessed resources.

Advanced Navigation Features

1. **Audience Targeting**:

SharePoint allows you to target specific navigation links to certain groups or users.

   o In the **Navigation Settings**, enable audience targeting for a link.

   o Assign it to specific user groups, ensuring that users only see relevant links.

2. **Breadcrumb Navigation**:

Breadcrumb trails show users their current location within a site and help them backtrack efficiently.

   o This feature is often automatically enabled, but you can configure it in **Navigation Settings**.

3. **Using Mega Menus**:

For complex sites with extensive content, Mega Menus provide a visually rich, dropdown-style navigation experience.

   o Available in modern SharePoint sites, Mega Menus allow you to organize multiple levels of links under expandable headers.

Common Challenges and How to Address Them

1. **Broken Links**:

    Ensure that all URLs are correct and updated. Test links periodically to prevent frustration.

2. **Inconsistent Navigation Across Sites**:

    If using Hub Sites, unify navigation by enabling a shared menu for all associated sites.

3. **Overcomplicated Menus**:

    If users report difficulty finding content, consider simplifying the menu or providing a site map.

Final Thoughts

Customizing navigation menus in SharePoint is a powerful way to create a user-centric experience. Whether you're managing a small team site or a large organizational hub, taking the time to design thoughtful, intuitive menus will pay off in improved efficiency and satisfaction. By leveraging advanced features like audience targeting and Mega Menus, you can further tailor the experience to your team's unique needs.

Start exploring the customization options today, and transform your SharePoint site into a streamlined, accessible workspace!

6.3 Automating Workflows

6.3.1 Introduction to Power Automate

Automating workflows in SharePoint can significantly streamline business processes, improve efficiency, and reduce the risk of manual errors. One of the most powerful tools available for automation in the Microsoft ecosystem is **Power Automate** (formerly Microsoft Flow). This platform enables users to create automated workflows between their favorite apps and services to synchronize files, get notifications, collect data, and more. In this section, we'll explore the fundamentals of Power Automate and how it integrates seamlessly with SharePoint to enhance your team's productivity.

What is Power Automate?

Power Automate is a cloud-based service that helps users automate repetitive tasks and business processes. It allows users of varying technical expertise to design workflows— known as **flows**—that connect different applications and systems. With Power Automate, users can:

- **Trigger actions based on events** (e.g., when a file is uploaded or updated).

- **Collect and analyze data** from multiple sources.

- **Send notifications or approvals** through integrated services like Microsoft Teams or Outlook.

- **Automate document management** tasks like file archiving and sharing.

By leveraging Power Automate within SharePoint, organizations can unlock its full potential for collaboration and process optimization.

Types of Flows in Power Automate

Understanding the different types of flows is essential before diving into SharePoint-specific use cases. Power Automate offers three primary types of flows:

1. **Automated Flows**

   These flows are triggered by specific events, such as when a new file is created in a SharePoint document library or when a list item is updated. They are ideal for automating repetitive tasks like document approvals or sending email alerts.

2. **Instant Flows**

   Triggered manually by the user, these flows are perfect for on-demand actions, such as generating a report or sending a notification to a specific team member. Instant flows can be launched directly from the SharePoint interface or the Power Automate app.

3. **Scheduled Flows**

   Scheduled flows run at predefined intervals, making them useful for routine maintenance tasks such as archiving older documents or generating weekly reports.

4. **Business Process Flows**

   These flows guide users through a predefined process to ensure consistency and compliance. For example, a hiring process flow might involve steps for reviewing resumes, conducting interviews, and sending offers.

Key Benefits of Using Power Automate in SharePoint

1. **Increased Efficiency**

   Automating repetitive tasks frees up valuable time for employees to focus on higher-value activities.

2. **Improved Accuracy**

   Automation reduces the likelihood of errors caused by manual data entry or inconsistent processes.

3. **Enhanced Collaboration**

   Automations such as approval workflows streamline communication between team members, ensuring everyone is on the same page.

4. **Scalability**

   Workflows can be scaled to accommodate larger teams or more complex processes without additional overhead.

Common SharePoint Use Cases for Power Automate

1. **Approval Workflows**

   Automate the approval of documents or list items by routing them to designated approvers via email or Microsoft Teams.

2. **Document Notifications**

   Notify team members when a new file is uploaded, a document is updated, or specific changes occur in a SharePoint library.

3. **Data Collection and Analysis**

   Automatically gather responses from forms and populate them into SharePoint lists for easy analysis.

4. **Content Archival**

   Move outdated files or list items to a designated archive location based on predefined conditions.

5. **Task Assignment**

   Create and assign tasks in Planner or Teams based on updates to SharePoint lists or libraries.

Building Your First SharePoint Flow with Power Automate

Let's walk through a simple example to help you get started with Power Automate: automating a document approval process.

1. **Access Power Automate**

- o Navigate to the Microsoft 365 app launcher and select **Power Automate**. Alternatively, you can access it directly from your SharePoint site by selecting **Automate > Power Automate** from a list or library menu.

2. **Create a New Flow**

- o In Power Automate, click **Create** and select **Automated Cloud Flow**.
- o Name your flow (e.g., "Document Approval Workflow").
- o Choose a trigger. For this example, select **When a file is created or modified (properties only)** for SharePoint.

3. **Configure the Trigger**

- o Enter the SharePoint site URL and select the relevant document library.

4. **Add an Action**

- o Add a new step by clicking **+ New Step**.
- o Search for "Start and wait for an approval" in the action menu.
- o Configure the approval process by specifying approvers and customizing the approval message.

5. **Set Conditions**

- o Use a **Condition** action to define what happens after approval or rejection. For example:
  - If approved, move the document to a designated folder.
  - If rejected, notify the document owner via email.

6. **Save and Test the Flow**

- o Save your flow and test it by uploading a file to the selected library.
- o Monitor the flow's progress in the Power Automate dashboard to ensure it functions as expected.

Best Practices for Using Power Automate with SharePoint

1. **Plan Your Workflow**

   Before creating a flow, map out the process on paper or using a tool like Lucidchart. This helps ensure that all steps are accounted for.

2. **Test Thoroughly**

   Run tests on your flow with sample data to identify and fix potential issues before deployment.

3. **Use Templates**

   Power Automate provides prebuilt templates for common workflows, saving you time and effort.

4. **Monitor and Optimize**

   Regularly review your flows to identify bottlenecks or opportunities for improvement. Use Power Automate analytics to track performance.

5. **Stay Secure**

   Ensure that your workflows adhere to your organization's security policies, especially when sharing data between applications.

Conclusion

Power Automate is a game-changing tool that empowers SharePoint users to streamline processes, reduce manual effort, and improve collaboration. Whether you're automating simple notifications or designing complex approval workflows, Power Automate offers the flexibility to meet your needs. By mastering its capabilities, you can unlock new levels of productivity and innovation within your SharePoint environment.

In the next section, we will explore **Common Workflow Examples**, providing detailed use cases to inspire your automation journey.

6.3.2 Common Workflow Examples

Automating workflows in SharePoint is a powerful way to streamline processes, reduce manual effort, and ensure consistency across tasks. In this section, we will explore some common workflow examples that can be implemented using SharePoint and Power Automate. These examples are designed to address frequent business needs and can serve as templates for creating your own custom workflows.

1. Approval Workflow

One of the most widely used workflows in SharePoint is the approval workflow. This process allows users to submit documents or items for review and approval by designated approvers.

How it Works:

- **Trigger:** A document is uploaded to a library or an item is created in a list.

- **Actions:**

    o The approver receives a notification via email or Microsoft Teams.

    o The approver can review the item and provide feedback or approve/reject it.

    o Based on the decision, the workflow can either move the item to a final folder, notify the submitter, or request additional changes.

Use Cases:

- Approving leave requests in an HR system.

- Reviewing marketing materials before publication.

- Getting sign-offs for contracts or project proposals.

Tips for Implementation:

- Use Power Automate's pre-built "Start an approval" action for seamless integration.

- Configure reminders for approvers to prevent delays.

2. Document Review and Expiry Notifications

Many organizations deal with documents that require periodic reviews or have expiration dates, such as policies, contracts, or licenses. Automating these notifications ensures that no critical dates are missed.

How it Works:

- **Trigger:** A document's review date or expiry date is approaching.
- **Actions:**
  - A reminder email is sent to the document owner or relevant stakeholders.
  - The workflow can also assign tasks for review or renewal.

Use Cases:

- Contract renewal alerts for procurement teams.
- Policy updates for compliance departments.
- Certification expirations for employee records.

Tips for Implementation:

- Add a metadata column for review dates in your document library.
- Use the "Delay until" action in Power Automate to schedule reminders.

3. Employee Onboarding Workflow

SharePoint can automate the onboarding process, ensuring new hires receive the necessary resources and complete their tasks efficiently.

How it Works:

- **Trigger:** A new employee is added to an HR SharePoint list.

- **Actions:**

  o Automatically create a personalized onboarding checklist.

  o Notify IT to set up accounts and equipment.

  o Provide the new hire with links to relevant documents, training modules, and policies.

Use Cases:

- Streamlining IT setup requests for new employees.

- Ensuring consistency in onboarding across departments.

- Reducing manual follow-ups by HR teams.

Tips for Implementation:

- Combine SharePoint with Microsoft Forms to collect employee details.

- Use Power Automate to assign tasks in Microsoft Planner.

---

4. Help Desk Ticketing Workflow

Organizations often use SharePoint to manage help desk requests for IT, facilities, or other support functions. Automating this process ensures requests are routed and resolved promptly.

How it Works:

- **Trigger:** A user submits a help desk request via a SharePoint form or list.

- **Actions:**

  o Assign the ticket to the appropriate support team or individual.

  o Notify the requester of the ticket status.

  o Update the ticket's status as it moves through the resolution stages.

Use Cases:

- IT support ticket tracking.

- Facilities maintenance requests.

- Customer service inquiries.

Tips for Implementation:

- Use SharePoint list views to display tickets by status or priority.

- Integrate with Microsoft Teams for real-time updates.

---

5. Meeting and Event Scheduling Workflow

SharePoint workflows can simplify the process of scheduling meetings or events, especially when multiple stakeholders are involved.

How it Works:

- **Trigger:** A meeting request form is submitted in SharePoint.

- **Actions:**

  o Automatically check availability of key participants using Outlook integration.

  o Send calendar invitations and include links to relevant documents or agendas.

  o Remind participants of the meeting or event.

Use Cases:

- Scheduling project kick-off meetings.

- Organizing company-wide training sessions.

- Planning social or team-building events.

Tips for Implementation:

- Leverage the "Get events" and "Create event" actions in Power Automate for seamless calendar integration.

- Use custom SharePoint forms for capturing event details.

---

6. Expense Approval Workflow

Managing expense claims manually can be tedious and prone to errors. Automating this process with SharePoint ensures faster approvals and better tracking.

How it Works:

- **Trigger:** An employee submits an expense claim through a SharePoint list or form.
- **Actions:**
    - Route the claim to the manager for approval.
    - Notify the finance team for reimbursement.
    - Track the status of claims in a centralized dashboard.

Use Cases:

- Employee travel expense claims.
- Office supply purchases.
- Training or conference fee reimbursements.

Tips for Implementation:

- Use metadata to categorize expenses by type or department.
- Automate notifications for pending claims to managers.

---

7. Content Publishing Workflow

For teams managing websites or intranets, SharePoint workflows can streamline the content publishing process.

How it Works:

- **Trigger:** A draft page or article is submitted for review.
- **Actions:**
  - Notify editors to review the content.
  - Once approved, move the content to the published state.
  - Notify stakeholders or teams about the new publication.

Use Cases:

- Publishing internal newsletters or announcements.
- Managing blog content on the company intranet.
- Updating training materials or FAQs.

Tips for Implementation:

- Use SharePoint's version history to track changes.
- Implement multi-level approvals for sensitive content.

Best Practices for Workflow Automation

- **Plan Before You Automate:** Clearly define the process you want to automate, including triggers, actions, and outcomes.
- **Test Thoroughly:** Run test scenarios to ensure workflows perform as expected before deploying them.
- **Leverage Pre-Built Templates:** Power Automate offers a wide range of workflow templates to get you started quickly.
- **Monitor and Optimize:** Regularly review automated workflows to identify areas for improvement or to adapt to changing needs.

Automating workflows in SharePoint can transform how your organization operates, enabling greater efficiency and collaboration. With these examples as a starting point, you can customize workflows to meet your specific business requirements.

CHAPTER VII
Advanced Features

7.1 Integrating with Power BI

7.1.1 Embedding Reports in SharePoint

Integrating Power BI with SharePoint allows organizations to leverage powerful data visualization and business intelligence tools directly within their collaborative environments. By embedding Power BI reports into SharePoint, users can streamline access to crucial insights without switching between multiple platforms. This integration boosts productivity and enhances decision-making by bringing data to the forefront of team collaboration.

In this section, we'll explore how to embed Power BI reports into SharePoint step by step, cover the key benefits of this integration, and highlight best practices for ensuring a seamless experience for all users.

Understanding Power BI and SharePoint Integration

Power BI is a leading tool for creating interactive and visually engaging reports and dashboards. It allows businesses to analyze data from various sources and present it in a way that's easy to understand. SharePoint, as a collaboration platform, serves as a hub for teams to manage files, share knowledge, and coordinate tasks. Combining these tools means your team can view and interact with vital data insights directly within the SharePoint environment.

Embedding Power BI reports in SharePoint requires two main components:

1. **A Published Power BI Report** – Reports created in Power BI Desktop or Power BI Service must be published to the Power BI Service.

2. **A SharePoint Online Site** – Embedding is supported in SharePoint Online, where web parts and integration features are readily available.

Step-by-Step Guide to Embedding Power BI Reports in SharePoint

1. Prepare Your Power BI Report

- **Create a Report:** Use Power BI Desktop to create an engaging report. Include charts, tables, and visualizations that address your team's specific needs.

- **Publish the Report:** Save and publish the report to the Power BI Service. Ensure the report is saved in a workspace where you can manage sharing and permissions.

2. Get the Embed Link

- Open the Power BI Service and navigate to the report you want to embed.

- Click on the **File** menu and select **Embed in SharePoint Online** to generate the embed link.

- Copy the link provided. This URL will be used to insert the report into your SharePoint page.

3. Add a Power BI Web Part in SharePoint

- Open your SharePoint Online site and navigate to the page where you want to embed the report.

- Click on **Edit Page** to open the page editor.

- Choose the section where you want to insert the report and click on the **+ Add Web Part** button.

- Search for **Power BI** in the available web parts and select it.

4. Embed the Report

- Paste the embed link you copied earlier into the web part configuration panel.

- Adjust the display settings to suit your needs, such as the height and width of the report.

- Save or publish the SharePoint page to make the embedded report visible to users.

Benefits of Embedding Power BI Reports in SharePoint

1. **Centralized Data Access:** Teams can access real-time insights without leaving SharePoint, making it easier to incorporate data into daily workflows.

2. **Enhanced Collaboration:** Embedded reports foster collaboration by allowing teams to discuss insights and strategies directly within SharePoint.

3. **Improved Decision-Making:** With key metrics readily available, teams can make informed decisions faster.

4. **Streamlined User Experience:** Reducing the need to switch between platforms enhances productivity and user satisfaction.

Best Practices for Embedding Power BI Reports

1. Optimize Report Design

Ensure your Power BI reports are easy to read and navigate. Use filters, slicers, and clear visualizations to help users quickly find the insights they need.

2. Manage Permissions Carefully

Embedding a Power BI report in SharePoint does not override Power BI's permissions. Users must have access to the report in Power BI Service to view it in SharePoint. Regularly audit permissions to ensure only authorized users have access.

3. Test the Embedded Report

Before publishing the page, test the embedded report to ensure it loads correctly, displays the intended data, and allows for interactivity if applicable.

4. Provide Training and Documentation

Not all users may be familiar with Power BI. Provide basic training and create a guide to help them understand how to interact with the embedded reports effectively.

Troubleshooting Common Issues

1. Report Fails to Load

- Ensure the user has the appropriate permissions in both Power BI Service and SharePoint.

- Check that the embed link is correct and hasn't been modified.

2. Interactivity Isn't Working

- Some interactive features may require additional configurations. Refer to Power BI documentation for advanced embedding options.

3. Performance Issues

- Optimize the Power BI report by minimizing the number of visuals and ensuring the underlying data model is efficient.

- Verify network connectivity, as embedding relies on stable access to the Power BI Service.

Embedding Power BI reports into SharePoint transforms how teams interact with data, making analytics accessible and actionable. With proper setup and thoughtful implementation, this integration can become a cornerstone of your team's collaboration strategy.

7.1.2 Setting Up Data Connections

Integrating Power BI with SharePoint involves establishing data connections to effectively pull information from various sources into Power BI. These data connections form the backbone of dynamic, interactive reports that provide insights directly within your SharePoint environment. In this section, we'll walk through the process of setting up data connections, best practices for maintaining them, and resolving potential issues.

Understanding Data Sources Compatible with Power BI

Power BI supports a wide range of data sources, enabling you to connect SharePoint with both internal and external systems. Common sources include:

- **SharePoint Lists and Libraries:** These provide structured data like inventory logs, project timelines, and contact lists.

- **Excel Files:** Often stored within SharePoint document libraries, Excel files can serve as input for detailed analysis.

- **SQL Databases:** For enterprise-level data, SQL databases allow seamless integration.

- **Other Microsoft Services:** Tools like Dynamics 365, Azure, and Teams also integrate natively.

- **External Data Sources:** REST APIs, cloud-based databases, and third-party applications can also connect via Power BI.

Step-by-Step Guide to Setting Up Data Connections

1. Prepare Your Data in SharePoint

Before you establish a connection, ensure that your SharePoint data is well-organized and ready for integration. This involves:

- **Cleaning Data:** Remove duplicates and ensure consistent formatting.

- **Structuring Lists and Libraries:** Use appropriate column types and metadata for easy filtering.

- **Setting Permissions:** Confirm that users accessing Power BI reports have the required permissions in SharePoint.

2. Access Power BI Desktop

Power BI Desktop is the primary tool for setting up data connections. Download and install it if you haven't already.

1. **Open Power BI Desktop**

   Launch the application to start creating a new report or editing an existing one.

2. **Connect to SharePoint Online**

- o Click **Home > Get Data** in the toolbar.

- o Choose **SharePoint Online List** or **Web** as the data source, depending on your needs.

- o Enter the URL of your SharePoint site. For example:

- o https://yourcompany.sharepoint.com/sites/yoursite

- o Authenticate with your Microsoft 365 credentials.

3. Load and Transform Data

Power BI allows you to preview and manipulate data before loading it into your workspace.

- Use the **Query Editor** to:

  - o Filter rows or columns.

  - o Remove unnecessary columns to reduce dataset size.

  - o Create calculated columns for derived insights.

4. Establish Data Relationships

If pulling data from multiple sources, establish relationships between tables for cohesive reporting.

- Navigate to the **Model View** and drag connections between datasets.

- Define cardinality (e.g., one-to-many) to reflect the data structure accurately.

5. Visualize Data in Power BI

Once the connection is live, use Power BI's visualizations to represent your data.

- Drag fields onto the canvas to create charts, graphs, and tables.

- Add slicers to allow users to filter data dynamically.

Best Practices for Data Connections

To maintain efficient and reliable data connections, follow these best practices:

1. **Optimize Data Volume:**

2. Large datasets can slow down performance. Use Power BI's filtering and aggregation features to reduce data size.

3. **Schedule Data Refreshes:**

   o   Set up automatic refresh intervals to keep reports up-to-date.

   o   Use the **Power BI Service** to manage refresh schedules.

4. **Secure Connections:**

   o   Use HTTPS for all SharePoint URLs to ensure encrypted communication.

   o   Implement role-based permissions in Power BI and SharePoint for data security.

5. **Monitor Data Integrity:**

   Periodically validate data to ensure that connections are not broken due to changes in SharePoint lists or libraries.

Troubleshooting Data Connection Issues

Sometimes, issues may arise during or after setting up data connections. Below are common problems and their solutions:

Authentication Errors

- **Problem:** Power BI cannot authenticate your credentials.

- **Solution:** Ensure that your Microsoft 365 account has sufficient permissions for the SharePoint site. Re-authenticate if necessary.

Data Mismatch or Missing Columns

- **Problem:** Data in Power BI doesn't match what's in SharePoint.

- **Solution:** Check if any recent changes were made to the SharePoint list structure. Refresh the data source and update queries.

Slow Performance

- **Problem:** Reports load slowly or time out.

- **Solution:** Optimize the query by filtering data and reducing unnecessary columns. Consider splitting data into smaller tables.

Connection Loss

- **Problem:** Power BI cannot connect to SharePoint.

- **Solution:** Verify that the SharePoint site URL is correct and accessible. Check network connectivity and SharePoint service status.

Enhancing SharePoint Reports with Power BI Features

Once your data connections are set, leverage advanced Power BI features to make your reports more impactful:

1. **Interactive Dashboards:**

   Add buttons, bookmarks, and tooltips to create an intuitive user experience.

2. **Custom Visualizations:**

   Explore Power BI Marketplace to integrate advanced visuals like heatmaps or KPIs.

3. **Row-Level Security (RLS):**

   Use RLS to restrict data access based on user roles, ensuring that team members only see data relevant to them.

4. **Embed Reports in SharePoint:**

   o Publish your Power BI report.

   o Use the **Power BI Web Part** in SharePoint to embed the report seamlessly on a SharePoint page.

Case Study: Real-World Application

To illustrate the benefits of integrating Power BI with SharePoint, consider this example:

- A marketing team uses SharePoint to manage campaign data, including budgets and performance metrics.

- By connecting SharePoint with Power BI, the team creates an interactive dashboard showing:

  o Budget allocation across campaigns.

  o Real-time performance metrics like ROI and conversion rates.

  o Historical trends for strategic decision-making.

This integration reduces manual reporting effort and provides a centralized view of campaign success.

Setting up data connections between Power BI and SharePoint unlocks powerful capabilities for data visualization and decision-making. By following the steps and best practices outlined above, you can transform SharePoint data into actionable insights, empowering your team to work smarter and faster.

7.2 External Sharing and Collaboration

7.2.1 Sharing with External Users

Sharing content with external users is one of SharePoint's most valuable features, enabling organizations to collaborate beyond their internal teams. This capability allows users to securely share documents, libraries, or even entire sites with clients, contractors, or partners. Properly configuring and managing external sharing ensures that sensitive data remains protected while facilitating seamless collaboration. In this section, we will explore the steps, best practices, and potential challenges of sharing with external users.

Understanding External Sharing in SharePoint

External sharing in SharePoint enables users outside your organization's Microsoft 365 environment to access selected content. These users do not need a Microsoft 365 account; they can interact with your shared content through a secure invitation link or guest account. External sharing can be implemented at multiple levels:

- **Individual Files or Folders:** Specific documents or folders can be shared without granting broader access to libraries or sites.

- **Document Libraries:** Share entire libraries to provide access to all documents within them.

- **SharePoint Sites:** Grant access to entire sites when ongoing, holistic collaboration is required.

By default, external sharing is controlled at both the tenant and site levels. Administrators must configure these permissions to align with organizational policies.

Enabling External Sharing

Before sharing with external users, ensure external sharing is enabled for your SharePoint environment:

1. **Verify Tenant-Level Settings:**

   o   Navigate to the Microsoft 365 Admin Center.

   o   Go to **Settings > Org Settings > Services > SharePoint**.

   o   Ensure external sharing is enabled, and configure the appropriate settings (e.g., allow sharing only with authenticated users).

2. **Adjust Site-Level Permissions:**

   o   Open the SharePoint admin center and select the site collection.

   o   Go to **Sharing Settings**, and specify whether external sharing is allowed for the site.

Sharing Content with External Users

Once external sharing is enabled, users can share content using the following methods:

Sharing Individual Files and Folders

1. **Navigate to the Content:**

   Open the SharePoint document library containing the file or folder you want to share.

2. **Select the Item to Share:**

   Click on the ellipsis (...) next to the item and choose **Share**.

3. **Create a Sharing Link:**

   In the sharing dialog box, select the type of link:

   o   **People with the link:** No sign-in required (least secure).

   o   **People in your organization with the link:** Only internal users can access it.

   o   **Specific people:** Only designated recipients can open the link.

4. **Set Permissions:**

Define whether recipients can **View** or **Edit** the content.

5. **Send the Invitation:**

   Enter the recipient's email address, add an optional message, and click **Send**.

Sharing an Entire Document Library

1. **Open the Document Library:**
   Access the library from your site's navigation pane.

2. **Click the Share Option:**
   Use the **Share** button at the top right corner.

3. **Configure the Permissions:**
   Follow the same steps as file-level sharing, ensuring appropriate access levels.

Sharing a SharePoint Site

1. **Go to Site Settings:**
   Access the gear icon and click on **Site Permissions**.

2. **Invite External Users:**
   Click **Share Site**, add email addresses, and select the permission level (e.g., Read, Edit).

3. **Send the Invitation:**
   External users will receive an email with instructions to access the site.

Managing External Users

Once users have been granted access, administrators should actively monitor and manage their permissions:

- **Review Guest Access Regularly:**
  Periodically audit external user permissions to ensure they only access what is necessary. Remove users who no longer need access.

- **Modify Permissions When Needed:**
  Use the **Site Permissions** settings to adjust roles or revoke access as projects evolve.

- **Leverage Expiration Policies:**
  Set expiration dates for sharing links to limit long-term access.

Security Best Practices for External Sharing

While external sharing can boost productivity, it also introduces security risks. Implement the following best practices to protect your data:

- **Use Conditional Access Policies:**
  Require external users to authenticate with multifactor authentication (MFA) before accessing shared content.

- **Restrict Sharing Capabilities:**
  Limit sharing permissions to specific roles (e.g., site owners) to prevent accidental data exposure.

- **Enable Alerts:**
  Configure alerts for unusual activity, such as mass downloads or access attempts from unfamiliar locations.

- **Use Sensitivity Labels:**
  Apply labels to classify documents based on sensitivity and automatically enforce sharing restrictions.

Common Challenges in External Sharing

While SharePoint's external sharing is intuitive, users may encounter challenges:

1. **Access Denied Errors:**
   Occurs when external users lack permissions or when site-level sharing settings are restrictive.

2. **Lost Sharing Links:**
   Users may accidentally delete shared links, requiring the creation of new ones.

3. **Account Issues:**
   External users without Microsoft accounts may face difficulties accessing shared content.

4. **Permission Sprawl:**
   Over time, excessive external sharing can lead to a cluttered and unmanageable permission structure.

To address these challenges, provide clear instructions to external users, and regularly train internal staff on best practices for managing access.

Real-World Use Cases

1. **Client Collaboration:**
   A marketing agency uses SharePoint to share project timelines and creative drafts with clients, allowing for real-time feedback.

2. **Vendor Management:**
   A manufacturing company provides suppliers with access to specific documents, such as blueprints and purchase orders, ensuring seamless communication.

3. **Cross-Company Projects:**
   A consulting firm collaborates with its partners by sharing secure SharePoint sites, enabling shared document editing and tracking.

Summary

External sharing in SharePoint is a powerful tool for fostering collaboration beyond organizational boundaries. By properly configuring permissions, adhering to security best practices, and managing user access, organizations can maximize the benefits of external sharing while mitigating risks. With careful implementation, SharePoint becomes a bridge for global teamwork, streamlining processes and enhancing productivity.

7.2.2 Security Considerations

External sharing and collaboration are powerful features of SharePoint, enabling organizations to work seamlessly with clients, partners, and vendors. However, these functionalities come with significant security considerations that must be addressed to protect sensitive information and ensure compliance with organizational and regulatory requirements. This section provides a comprehensive guide to understanding and implementing best practices for secure external collaboration in SharePoint.

1. Understanding Security Risks in External Sharing

External sharing inherently introduces potential risks, including:

- **Unauthorized Access**: Granting external users access to SharePoint sites and documents increases the possibility of unintended data exposure.

- **Data Breaches**: Without proper safeguards, external sharing can lead to the accidental or intentional leakage of sensitive information.

- **Non-Compliance**: Mismanagement of permissions or insufficient controls may result in violations of industry regulations, such as GDPR, HIPAA, or ISO standards.

- **Phishing and Malware Threats**: External users may inadvertently or maliciously introduce security threats through uploaded files or email links.

Understanding these risks underscores the importance of establishing robust security practices.

2. Configuring Secure External Sharing in SharePoint

SharePoint offers a range of tools and settings to manage and secure external sharing. Below are key considerations and steps:

2.1 Defining External Sharing Policies

Start by setting clear policies at both the organizational and site levels:

- **Organization-Level Settings**: Admins can configure whether external sharing is allowed across the tenant and establish global rules.

- **Site-Level Controls**: SharePoint enables site-specific sharing settings, allowing admins to customize permissions for each project or collaboration.

2.2 Limiting External Access

SharePoint provides options to restrict access based on user roles or organizational needs:

- **Allowing Only Specific Domains**: Restrict external sharing to users from pre-approved domains.

- **Guest Access Levels**: Configure granular guest access, such as view-only permissions or blocking downloads.

2.3 Setting Expiration Dates for Shared Links

To minimize long-term exposure, enforce expiration dates for all external sharing links. This ensures that access is temporary and aligned with project timelines.

2.4 Enforcing Authentication

Require external users to authenticate with their Microsoft account or another verified identity provider. Authentication prevents anonymous access and improves accountability.

---

3. Best Practices for Secure Collaboration

3.1 Principle of Least Privilege

Grant external users the minimum permissions necessary to complete their tasks. Avoid providing full site access unless absolutely required.

3.2 Regularly Review Access

Conduct periodic audits of external user permissions. Revoke access for users who no longer require it or whose collaboration period has ended.

3.3 Enable Data Loss Prevention (DLP) Policies

Use DLP policies to detect and prevent the sharing of sensitive data, such as financial information, customer records, or intellectual property. These policies can automatically block or notify users attempting to share restricted content.

3.4 Monitor Activity Logs

Enable and review audit logs to track external user activities, including document access and modifications. Monitoring ensures early detection of suspicious behavior.

4. Advanced Security Features in SharePoint

SharePoint integrates with Microsoft's advanced security tools, providing additional layers of protection:

4.1 Microsoft Defender for Office 365

- Scans for malicious files and links shared externally.

- Provides alerts for potential threats or unusual activities.

4.2 Azure Active Directory (Azure AD) Conditional Access

- Controls access based on conditions such as user location, device status, or risk profile.

- Blocks or restricts access for high-risk activities.

4.3 Encryption and Secure File Sharing

All files in SharePoint are encrypted at rest and in transit. For additional security, use Microsoft Information Protection (MIP) to apply encryption and sensitivity labels to shared content.

4.4 Multi-Factor Authentication (MFA)

Enforce MFA for all external users. Requiring a second verification step reduces the risk of unauthorized access even if credentials are compromised.

---

5. Regulatory and Compliance Considerations

Organizations must ensure that their external sharing practices comply with relevant laws and standards:

- **GDPR (General Data Protection Regulation)**: For organizations operating in the EU, ensure that external sharing complies with data protection requirements.

- **HIPAA (Health Insurance Portability and Accountability Act)**: Protect healthcare-related information shared externally.

- **Industry Standards**: Follow ISO 27001 or similar frameworks to maintain a secure environment for external collaboration.

Using SharePoint's compliance features, such as retention labels, eDiscovery, and audit logs, can help demonstrate adherence to these regulations.

6. Educating Users on Security Best Practices

External sharing security is only as strong as the users implementing it. Conduct training and awareness sessions for employees to:

- Recognize potential phishing attempts.

- Avoid sharing sensitive data with unauthorized users.

- Properly use SharePoint's sharing and permissions features.

Encourage a culture of security mindfulness among all stakeholders.

7. Balancing Security and Collaboration

While security is critical, it should not come at the expense of usability. Overly restrictive policies can hinder productivity and discourage external collaboration. Strike a balance by:

- Collaborating with stakeholders to understand project needs.

- Testing security configurations to ensure they support seamless workflows.

- Continuously refining policies based on user feedback and evolving risks.

Conclusion

Security considerations for external sharing and collaboration in SharePoint are multifaceted but manageable with the right tools and practices. By implementing a robust strategy, organizations can confidently leverage SharePoint's external sharing capabilities without compromising data integrity or compliance. Following these guidelines will help you maximize the benefits of collaboration while minimizing potential risks.

7.3 Mobile Access and Applications

7.3.1 Using the SharePoint Mobile App

In today's fast-paced work environment, mobile access is a crucial feature of any collaboration tool. SharePoint's mobile app allows users to stay connected to their files, sites, and workflows from anywhere. This section explores the features, benefits, and practical tips for using the SharePoint mobile app effectively.

Overview of the SharePoint Mobile App

The SharePoint mobile app, available for both iOS and Android devices, is designed to bring the power of SharePoint to your fingertips. The app provides streamlined access to:

- **Sites:** Quickly navigate to your frequently used SharePoint sites.

- **Documents:** View, edit, and share files directly from your mobile device.

- **News and Updates:** Stay informed with real-time updates and news posts.

- **Search and Discover:** Use the robust search feature to locate files, lists, or people within your organization.

- **Offline Access:** Work with important documents even without an internet connection.

The app's intuitive interface ensures that both beginners and experienced users can easily adapt to its functionality.

Getting Started with the SharePoint Mobile App

1. Downloading and Installing the App

To start, download the app from the Apple App Store or Google Play Store.

- Search for **Microsoft SharePoint** and install the application.

- Once installed, launch the app and sign in using your Microsoft 365 account credentials.

2. Setting Up Your Profile

Upon signing in, you'll be prompted to customize your profile. Add a profile picture and update any necessary information to improve collaboration and visibility across your organization.

3. Granting Permissions

The app may request permissions to access your device's storage, camera, and notifications. These permissions are necessary for features such as uploading files, scanning documents, and receiving updates.

Key Features of the SharePoint Mobile App

1. Accessing SharePoint Sites

The app provides easy navigation to your sites:

- The **Home Tab** displays your frequently accessed sites and recent activity.
- Use the **Search Bar** to locate specific sites.
- Bookmark essential sites for quicker access.

You can also customize your experience by rearranging your site list based on priority.

2. Managing Files on the Go

With the SharePoint mobile app, you can:

- **Open and Edit Documents:** View files directly in the app or edit them using integrated tools like Microsoft Word, Excel, or PowerPoint.
- **Share Files:** Generate shareable links or email attachments directly from the app.
- **Upload New Documents:** Take pictures or upload existing files from your device.

3. Real-Time Collaboration

Collaborating on documents is seamless:

- Use **Comments** to communicate with team members on specific files.

- View **Version History** to track changes and revert to previous versions when necessary.

- Access **Co-Authoring** features to edit documents simultaneously with colleagues.

4. Staying Updated with News and Announcements

The app ensures you stay informed with:

- A **News Tab** that highlights updates from your organization.

- Push notifications for new posts, ensuring you never miss critical updates.

- The ability to comment or like news articles to engage with content directly.

5. Utilizing Search and Discovery

The search functionality is robust and user-friendly:

- Search by keywords to find documents, lists, or colleagues.

- Use **Filters** to narrow down search results based on file type, author, or date.

- Discover related content or trending documents shared by your team.

Advanced Tips for Maximizing the App's Potential

1. Use Offline Mode for Productivity

Offline mode enables users to:

- Download essential files or site pages for offline access.

- Make changes to documents offline, which will sync automatically once you're connected to the internet.

This feature is particularly helpful for professionals working in areas with limited connectivity.

2. Leverage the Camera Integration

The app's camera integration allows you to:

- Scan documents and upload them directly to SharePoint.

- Capture photos of whiteboards or meeting notes and share them instantly with your team.

3. Customize Notifications

Set up tailored notifications to avoid information overload:

- Enable notifications for specific sites, libraries, or updates.

- Use **Do Not Disturb** settings during non-working hours for a better work-life balance.

Common Challenges and Solutions

1. Synchronization Issues

Sometimes, files or updates may not sync correctly. To resolve this:

- Ensure your app and operating system are up to date.

- Check your internet connection and refresh the app.

- Use the "Sync Now" button to manually trigger synchronization.

2. Storage Limitations on Mobile Devices

Storage constraints can affect file uploads. To optimize:

- Use the **Cloud Sync** feature to manage files without consuming local storage.

- Regularly clear cache and temporary files from the app settings.

3. Security Concerns

Mobile devices can be more vulnerable to security threats. Enhance security by:

- Enabling **Multi-Factor Authentication (MFA)** for your Microsoft account.

- Using app-specific passcodes or biometric authentication for added protection.

- Avoiding access to SharePoint on public Wi-Fi networks without a VPN.

Use Cases for the SharePoint Mobile App

1. Field Workers and Remote Teams

Field workers can instantly upload reports, images, or site inspections to SharePoint, ensuring real-time updates for the central team.

2. Executives and Managers

Leaders can review reports, approve workflows, or stay informed about project updates while on the move.

3. Sales and Client-Facing Teams

Sales professionals can access marketing materials, contracts, or client documents directly during meetings, enhancing efficiency and client satisfaction.

Conclusion

The SharePoint mobile app is a powerful tool for staying connected and productive, regardless of your location. By mastering its features, users can enhance their workflows, ensure real-time collaboration, and maintain seamless communication with their teams. With continuous updates and integration with Microsoft 365 tools, the SharePoint mobile app is an indispensable resource for modern professionals.

7.3.2 Mobile vs. Desktop Features

In today's fast-paced world, mobile access to SharePoint plays a vital role in ensuring productivity and seamless collaboration, regardless of location. While SharePoint's desktop version offers a more extensive set of features and tools, its mobile counterpart provides a streamlined, on-the-go experience tailored for smaller screens and touch interactions. Understanding the similarities and differences between these platforms is crucial to maximizing their potential in different scenarios.

Overview of Mobile Features

The SharePoint mobile app is designed to provide users with core functionalities in a user-friendly interface. It enables quick access to sites, documents, and collaboration tools while focusing on simplicity and usability. Here are the key features available in the mobile app:

- **Quick Access to Sites and Content:** Users can easily access frequently visited sites and libraries directly from the app's homepage. The search functionality helps locate specific files or resources swiftly.

- **Offline Access:** With mobile, you can download files for offline use, ensuring uninterrupted productivity even without an internet connection.

- **Push Notifications:** Stay updated with real-time alerts for document edits, comments, and other activities within your SharePoint sites.

- **Integration with Other Microsoft 365 Apps:** The app integrates seamlessly with mobile versions of Word, Excel, and Teams, enabling a unified workflow.

Key Differences Between Mobile and Desktop Features

1. Interface and Navigation

- **Desktop Version:** The desktop version offers a full-fledged interface with a wider screen layout, allowing detailed views of complex libraries, dashboards, and reports. Navigation menus, sidebars, and toolbars are accessible for advanced operations like managing permissions or configuring workflows.

- **Mobile Version:** The mobile app uses a compact design optimized for touch inputs. Navigation menus are condensed, and key features are grouped for ease of access on smaller screens. While it simplifies usage, some advanced settings and tools are unavailable.

2. File Management Capabilities

- **Desktop Version:** Desktop users can perform comprehensive file management tasks, such as batch uploads, version comparisons, and advanced metadata editing. The drag-and-drop feature simplifies organizing files into libraries.

- **Mobile Version:** File management on mobile is limited to viewing, uploading, and downloading individual files. Metadata editing is restricted, and certain file operations may require the desktop version.

3. Document Collaboration

- **Desktop Version:** Real-time co-authoring is more robust on the desktop, with features like in-line comments and advanced formatting tools in Word, Excel, or PowerPoint. Users can open multiple documents simultaneously, making comparisons easier.

- **Mobile Version:** Co-authoring is supported but can feel constrained due to limited screen space. Editing complex documents or adding detailed comments may be challenging on mobile devices.

4. Customization and Settings

- **Desktop Version:** SharePoint desktop offers extensive customization options, from site themes to page layouts and web part configurations. Administrators can configure permissions, manage workflows, and create automated processes.

- **Mobile Version:** Customization features are minimal on the mobile app. While users can access content and participate in discussions, administrative tasks like setting up permissions or editing web parts require a desktop environment.

5. Power BI Integration

- **Desktop Version:** The desktop version excels in displaying and managing embedded Power BI dashboards. Users can filter data, interact with visuals, and make adjustments directly from the site.

- **Mobile Version:** Power BI dashboards are accessible on mobile, but interactions are limited. Zooming and filtering data can feel constrained compared to the desktop experience.

6. Communication and Collaboration Tools

- **Desktop Version:** Desktop users have access to discussion boards, newsfeeds, and SharePoint calendars. These tools are tightly integrated with other Microsoft 365 applications like Outlook and Teams for seamless communication.

- **Mobile Version:** The mobile app supports basic collaboration features like commenting and accessing shared files. However, tools like discussion boards and newsfeeds are more intuitive and easier to manage on the desktop.

7. Offline Capabilities

- **Desktop Version:** Offline capabilities on the desktop are typically managed through OneDrive sync. Users can sync SharePoint libraries to their computers for offline editing and automatic synchronization when back online.

- **Mobile Version:** Offline access is simpler on mobile, with options to download specific files. However, syncing entire libraries for offline use is not supported, making it less practical for handling large volumes of data.

When to Use Mobile vs. Desktop

Mobile Use Cases:

- **On-the-Go Access:** Mobile is ideal for quickly reviewing documents, approving requests, or checking updates during meetings or travel.

- **Field Work:** Employees working in field operations, such as logistics or maintenance, can benefit from real-time access to manuals, schedules, or task updates.

- **Basic Collaboration:** Commenting on documents or responding to queries is efficient through the app.

Desktop Use Cases:

- **Complex Workflows:** Tasks such as setting up approval processes, creating custom dashboards, or managing large libraries are better suited for the desktop.

- **Detailed Document Editing:** Extensive edits, formatting, and design tasks are easier to accomplish on the desktop.

- **Advanced Reporting:** Viewing and interacting with Power BI reports or generating detailed analytics requires the full capabilities of the desktop version.

Best Practices for Using Mobile and Desktop Together

1. **Leverage Strengths:** Use mobile for quick tasks and on-the-go access, while reserving complex operations for the desktop.

2. **Sync Documents:** Ensure documents are synced across devices for uninterrupted access and continuity.

3. **Train Teams:** Provide training on the strengths and limitations of each platform to optimize workflows.

4. **Utilize Notifications:** Enable mobile push notifications to stay updated and address urgent issues promptly.

In conclusion, both the mobile app and desktop version of SharePoint serve distinct yet complementary roles. While the desktop version is indispensable for comprehensive management and customization, the mobile app ensures flexibility and accessibility. By understanding and leveraging their unique features, users can maximize productivity and enhance collaboration across their teams.

CHAPTER VIII
Maintaining Your SharePoint Environment

8.1 Monitoring Site Activity

8.1.1 Using SharePoint Analytics

SharePoint Analytics is an essential tool for monitoring the activity and performance of your SharePoint environment. By providing valuable insights into user behavior, content interaction, and overall site health, analytics helps administrators and site owners make informed decisions to optimize workflows, improve user experiences, and maintain a secure and efficient digital workspace.

Understanding SharePoint Analytics

At its core, SharePoint Analytics collects and displays data about how users interact with your SharePoint sites. It covers a range of metrics, including page views, active users, document downloads, and more. The analytics dashboard is accessible to users with administrative privileges and offers intuitive visuals that make complex data easy to interpret.

Key features of SharePoint Analytics include:

- **Site Usage Reports:** Displays data on user activity, such as the number of visits, unique viewers, and average time spent on a page or site.

- **File and Page Insights:** Provides details on the popularity of specific documents, pages, or libraries.

- **Shared Content Analysis:** Tracks how shared links are being accessed and identifies patterns in file sharing.

- **External Sharing Data:** Monitors interactions with external users to ensure compliance with security protocols.

Setting Up SharePoint Analytics

To begin using SharePoint Analytics, you must have the appropriate permissions. Generally, site administrators or owners can access the analytics dashboard directly from the SharePoint interface. Follow these steps to access it:

1. **Navigate to the Site Settings:**

   o Open the SharePoint site you want to analyze.

   o Click the gear icon in the upper-right corner and select **Site Contents** or **Site Settings** from the menu.

2. **Access the Analytics Dashboard:**

   o Under **Site Settings**, locate the **Site Usage** option.

   o Click it to open the analytics page, where you'll find key metrics and visualizations.

3. **Customize the Time Range:**

   o Most dashboards allow you to filter data by specific time ranges (e.g., last 7 days, 30 days, or a custom date range).

   o Use these filters to focus on the period of interest.

Interpreting Key Metrics

SharePoint Analytics provides a wealth of data, but understanding what these numbers mean is critical for making informed decisions. Let's break down some of the most important metrics:

1. **Unique Viewers:**

   o This metric shows how many distinct users have accessed your site during the selected time frame.

   o High numbers indicate strong engagement, while a decline may signal a need to refresh content or improve usability.

2. **Page Views:**

- o Tracks the total number of views for all pages on your site.

- o Pages with low views may require additional promotion or updates to increase relevance.

3. **Popular Content:**

- o Lists the most frequently accessed pages or documents.

- o Use this data to identify what content resonates with your audience and consider creating similar materials.

4. **File Activity:**

- o Monitors actions such as uploads, downloads, and edits on shared documents.

- o A surge in activity may indicate the need for additional storage or better version control.

5. **Average Time Spent Per User:**

- o Reflects how much time users spend engaging with your site.

- o Longer durations suggest effective content, while shorter visits may highlight usability issues.

Leveraging Analytics for Optimization

Once you've gathered data, the next step is to use these insights to enhance your SharePoint environment. Here are some actionable strategies:

1. **Improve Navigation:**

- o If analytics reveal that users are spending excessive time finding information, consider restructuring your navigation menus or implementing a search-friendly taxonomy.

2. **Update Underperforming Pages:**

- o Identify pages with low engagement and update their content or design to better meet user needs.

3. **Promote Popular Content:**

o   Share high-performing content with a broader audience via email campaigns, intranet announcements, or other communication channels.

4. **Monitor External Sharing:**

    o   Pay close attention to data about shared files to ensure sensitive information is accessed appropriately and complies with company policies.

5. **Allocate Resources Wisely:**

    o   Use engagement data to prioritize resource allocation, focusing on areas that generate the most impact.

Automating Reports with Power BI

For advanced users, integrating SharePoint Analytics with Power BI can offer even deeper insights. Power BI enables custom reporting and visualization, allowing you to merge SharePoint data with other business metrics for a comprehensive view.

Steps to Connect SharePoint and Power BI:

1. Open Power BI and navigate to the **Data Sources** section.

2. Select **SharePoint Online List** as your source.

3. Authenticate with your Microsoft account credentials.

4. Choose the desired lists or libraries to import data.

5. Customize dashboards to display the most relevant metrics.

Common Pitfalls and How to Avoid Them

While SharePoint Analytics is a powerful tool, there are some challenges to keep in mind:

1. **Overloading Users with Data:**

    o   Too many reports can overwhelm stakeholders. Focus on actionable insights that align with business goals.

2. **Ignoring Trends Over Time:**

    o   Isolated metrics may not provide the full picture. Regularly review long-term trends to identify patterns and opportunities.

3. **Failing to Address Privacy Concerns:**

   o Always respect user privacy when analyzing data. Follow organizational and legal guidelines to ensure compliance.

4. **Not Acting on Insights:**

   o Data is only valuable if it drives action. Regularly update workflows, content, or site structure based on analytics findings.

Final Thoughts

Using SharePoint Analytics is a critical component of maintaining an effective SharePoint environment. By leveraging its insights, administrators and site owners can proactively address challenges, enhance user engagement, and streamline operations. As you continue exploring SharePoint Analytics, remember to revisit your strategies regularly and adapt to changing user needs. This proactive approach will ensure your SharePoint environment remains a cornerstone of collaboration and productivity.

8.1.2 Understanding Site Usage Reports

Site usage reports in SharePoint are essential tools for administrators and site owners who want to evaluate how their sites are being utilized. These reports provide valuable insights into user engagement, popular content, and overall site activity, enabling better decision-making for improvements and optimizations. This section will explore what site usage reports are, the data they provide, and how to interpret and leverage them effectively.

What Are Site Usage Reports?

Site usage reports are analytics tools built into SharePoint that allow users to understand how their site is being accessed and interacted with. These reports help identify trends, monitor traffic, and measure the effectiveness of content and structure. By analyzing these reports, administrators can gain insights into:

- Which content is most accessed.

- User engagement levels.

- Patterns of site visits over time.

- Potential areas for improvement in navigation or design.

Accessing Site Usage Reports

To view site usage reports in SharePoint, follow these steps:

1. Navigate to the SharePoint site for which you want to view reports.

2. Click on the **Settings** gear icon in the upper right corner.

3. Select **Site usage** from the dropdown menu.

4. The site usage page will display various metrics, charts, and data summaries.

The reports are only available to site owners and administrators with appropriate permissions, ensuring that sensitive information is not disclosed to unauthorized users.

Key Metrics in Site Usage Reports

SharePoint site usage reports offer a wide array of metrics that provide a comprehensive picture of site activity. The following are some of the most critical metrics:

1. Unique Viewers

- Tracks the number of individual users who have accessed the site within a specific period (e.g., last 7 days, last 30 days).

- Helps assess the reach and popularity of the site.

2. Site Visits

- Measures the total number of visits, providing a broader view of site activity.

- Useful for understanding recurring engagement.

3. Popular Content

- Lists the pages, documents, or items that have received the most views or interactions.

- Helps determine which content is resonating with users and driving engagement.

4. Average Time Spent per User

- Indicates the average duration users spend on the site.

- A high average time suggests engaging and meaningful content, while a low average time might indicate issues like poor navigation or irrelevant content.

5. Shared with External Users

- Highlights content that has been shared with people outside the organization.

- Important for tracking external collaboration and ensuring compliance with security policies.

Interpreting Site Usage Data

1. Identifying Trends

By reviewing site usage over different time periods, you can identify patterns and trends. For instance, you may notice spikes in activity following announcements or the publication of new content. This insight can guide the timing of future updates or events.

2. Analyzing Content Effectiveness

Use the "Popular Content" metric to determine which pages or files are most accessed. If certain content is rarely visited, consider revising its placement, updating its information, or promoting it more effectively.

3. Evaluating User Engagement

The combination of metrics like "Unique Viewers" and "Average Time Spent per User" can indicate how well users are engaging with the site. Low engagement may signal issues such as confusing navigation, uninteresting content, or technical barriers.

4. Monitoring External Sharing

Keep an eye on the "Shared with External Users" data to ensure compliance with company policies. Frequent external sharing may require additional security measures or user training.

Leveraging Site Usage Reports for Improvements

1. Enhancing Content Strategy

- Focus on creating more of the content types that are popular among users.

- Regularly update existing content to keep it relevant and engaging.

2. Optimizing Navigation and Structure

- Use insights from site visits and popular content metrics to streamline site navigation.

- Ensure that frequently accessed content is easy to find.

3. Supporting Targeted Communication

- Identify user groups or departments that access specific content and tailor communications to their needs.

- Promote underused resources to boost awareness and usage.

4. Maintaining Site Performance

- High traffic to specific pages may require performance optimization to prevent slow load times.

- Regularly archive outdated content to ensure the site remains responsive.

Best Practices for Using Site Usage Reports

1. Set Benchmarks and Goals

Establish performance benchmarks based on initial site usage data and set clear goals for improvement. For example, aim to increase average time spent on the site by 10% over six months.

2. Monitor Regularly

Review site usage reports on a consistent basis (e.g., weekly or monthly). Regular monitoring helps identify issues early and track progress over time.

3. Combine with Other Tools

Integrate SharePoint usage data with tools like Power BI for advanced analytics and visualization. Combining data sources provides deeper insights and supports data-driven decisions.

4. Act on Feedback

Use the insights gained from site usage reports to make actionable changes. For example, if a document library is heavily used, consider adding quick links or making it more prominent on the homepage.

Challenges and Limitations

While site usage reports are invaluable, they have some limitations:

- **Data Retention**: SharePoint retains site usage data for a limited time (e.g., 90 days for some metrics), so historical analysis may be restricted.

- **Privacy Restrictions**: User-specific data may be anonymized or unavailable due to privacy policies, limiting detailed user behavior tracking.

- **Technical Barriers**: Interpreting data may require a learning curve, especially for non-technical users.

To overcome these challenges, consider complementing SharePoint analytics with external tools or collaborating with IT experts for deeper insights.

Conclusion

Understanding site usage reports is a critical skill for managing a successful SharePoint environment. These reports provide actionable insights into how your site is being utilized, allowing you to make data-driven improvements. By regularly analyzing usage metrics, interpreting trends, and acting on findings, you can enhance user engagement, streamline operations, and maintain a thriving SharePoint environment.

8.2 Troubleshooting Common Issues

8.2.1 Fixing Permissions Errors

Permissions errors are among the most common challenges faced by SharePoint users. These errors can disrupt collaboration, prevent access to critical files, and lead to confusion among team members. In this section, we will explore the causes of permissions errors, their potential impact, and step-by-step methods to identify and resolve these issues effectively.

Understanding Permissions in SharePoint

Before troubleshooting permissions errors, it is essential to understand how permissions work in SharePoint. SharePoint permissions are governed by a hierarchical structure that starts at the site level and cascades down to libraries, lists, folders, and individual items. Key components of SharePoint permissions include:

1. **Permission Levels**: These define what users can do within a site, such as viewing, editing, or contributing to content. Common permission levels include "Read," "Contribute," "Edit," and "Full Control."

2. **Groups and Roles**: Users are often grouped into predefined roles like "Owners," "Members," and "Visitors," each with specific permission levels.

3. **Inheritance**: Permissions can be inherited from parent elements, such as a library inheriting settings from its site. Breaking this inheritance allows customized permissions for specific items.

Misconfigurations or miscommunications within these components can lead to errors.

Common Causes of Permissions Errors

1. **Broken Inheritance**: When inheritance is broken at a specific level, users may lose or gain unintended permissions.

2. **User Misassignment**: Users might be assigned to incorrect groups or roles, causing access issues.

3. **Conflicting Permissions**: Overlapping permissions can create contradictions, such as a user being both granted and denied access to the same resource.

4. **External Sharing Mismanagement**: Inappropriate settings for external users can block or expose resources unintentionally.

5. **Changes to Group Membership**: When users are removed from groups or roles without updating permissions elsewhere, errors may occur.

6. **Expired Links or Access**: Time-sensitive sharing links may expire, leaving users unable to access files or folders.

Steps to Troubleshoot Permissions Errors

Follow these steps to diagnose and resolve permissions-related issues in SharePoint:

Step 1: Identify the Scope of the Problem

Start by determining the extent of the issue:

- **Who is affected?** Is it an individual, a group, or everyone accessing a resource?

- **What resource is impacted?** Identify the file, folder, library, or site in question.

- **When did the issue occur?** Recent changes to permissions, settings, or memberships might be the cause.

- **What error messages are shown?** SharePoint often provides descriptive messages like "Access Denied" or "You need permission to access this item."

Gathering this information helps narrow down the root cause.

Step 2: Review Permissions Settings

Navigate to the affected resource and check its current permissions:

1. **Open the Settings Panel**: For a site, click on the gear icon and select "Site Permissions." For a library or folder, use the "Manage Access" option.

2. **Check Group Memberships**: Verify which users or groups have been granted access and their associated permission levels.

3. **Inspect Inheritance**: Determine whether the resource inherits permissions from its parent. If inheritance is broken, review the customized permissions.

Step 3: Test User Access

Impersonate the user experiencing the issue:

1. **Use the "Check Permissions" Tool**: Available in the site or library settings, this tool shows the exact permissions a user has and their origin.

2. **Test with a Dummy Account**: Create a temporary account with identical permissions to replicate the problem.

Step 4: Resolve the Identified Issue

Based on your findings, apply the appropriate fixes:

Case 1: Reinstate Inheritance

If broken inheritance is causing the error:

- Navigate to the affected item.

- Select "Advanced Permissions Settings."

- Click on "Delete unique permissions" to reinstate inheritance from the parent.

Case 2: Correct User Assignment

If a user is in the wrong group:

- Navigate to "Site Permissions."

- Add the user to the correct group using the "Grant Permissions" button.

- Remove them from any conflicting groups.

Case 3: Resolve Conflicting Permissions

If permissions are contradictory:

- Use the "Check Permissions" tool to identify overlaps.

- Modify the permissions of the affected user or group to ensure consistency.

Case 4: Address External Sharing Issues

For external users:

- Confirm that external sharing is enabled in site settings.

- Resend a valid sharing link, ensuring it aligns with the required access level.

- Check the expiration date of the link and extend it if necessary.

Step 5: Test and Confirm Resolution

After making changes, re-test the user's access to ensure the problem is resolved. Communicate the outcome to the affected user(s) and provide guidance on how to avoid similar issues in the future.

Tips for Preventing Permissions Errors

1. **Standardize Permission Practices**: Use consistent roles and groups across your SharePoint environment to minimize confusion.

2. **Regularly Audit Permissions**: Periodically review and update permissions to ensure they align with organizational needs.

3. **Educate Team Members**: Train users on how permissions work and how to request changes when needed.

4. **Limit Customization**: Avoid excessive customization of permissions unless necessary. Use inheritance whenever possible.

5. **Monitor Changes**: Track changes to group memberships and permissions to anticipate potential issues.

Advanced Tools for Permissions Management

1. **PowerShell Scripts**: Use scripts to automate permissions management tasks, such as bulk updates or detailed audits.

2. **Microsoft Defender for Office 365**: Enhance security by identifying suspicious activities related to permissions changes.

3. **Third-Party Solutions**: Tools like ShareGate or AvePoint provide advanced features for managing and auditing permissions.

By following these guidelines, you can effectively resolve permissions errors in SharePoint, ensuring smooth and secure collaboration across your organization.

8.2.2 Recovering Deleted Files and Sites

One of SharePoint's greatest strengths is its ability to manage and safeguard your files and sites. However, mistakes can happen—files may be accidentally deleted, or entire sites may be removed without intending to do so. Fortunately, SharePoint provides robust tools to help users recover deleted files and even restore sites with minimal disruption. This section will walk you through the processes of recovering deleted content and provide best practices for minimizing data loss.

The Recycle Bin: A Safety Net for Deleted Items

When files or list items are deleted in SharePoint, they are not immediately lost. Instead, they are moved to the **Recycle Bin**, a temporary storage area that serves as the first line of recovery. Deleted items remain in the Recycle Bin for a configurable period, typically 93 days, before being permanently removed.

Steps to Recover Deleted Files from the Recycle Bin:

1. **Navigate to the Recycle Bin:**

   o   Go to your SharePoint site and click on the gear icon at the top-right corner.

   o   Select **Site Contents**, and then click on the **Recycle Bin** link in the top-right corner of the page.

2. **Locate the Deleted Item:**

   o   Browse or search for the file, folder, or list item you wish to recover.

   o   You can filter by deletion date or use the search bar to narrow down the results.

3. **Restore the Item:**

   o   Select the checkbox next to the item(s) you want to recover.

   o   Click **Restore**, and the selected items will be returned to their original location in the site.

Tips for Using the Recycle Bin Effectively:

- Regularly check the Recycle Bin to ensure no critical items are accidentally left to expire.

- Notify team members about the presence of the Recycle Bin, as many users are unaware of its functionality.

Second-Stage Recycle Bin: When Items Aren't Where You Expect

If you cannot find your deleted item in the primary Recycle Bin, it may have been moved to the **Second-Stage Recycle Bin**, which is accessible only to site administrators. This secondary bin holds items that users have deleted from the primary Recycle Bin and offers another chance to recover critical data.

Accessing the Second-Stage Recycle Bin:

1. As a site administrator, navigate to **Site Contents** and then to the primary Recycle Bin.

2. At the bottom of the Recycle Bin page, click on the link to the **Second-Stage Recycle Bin**.

3. Follow the same steps as above to locate and restore your item.

Recovering Deleted Sites

In addition to files and list items, entire sites can sometimes be deleted unintentionally. SharePoint's site recovery process depends on whether the site is part of a classic SharePoint structure or a modern hub-based architecture.

Recovering Modern Sites:

Modern SharePoint sites are typically part of Office 365 groups, which means they can be restored via the Microsoft 365 Admin Center. Here's how:

1. **Log into the Admin Center:**

   o As an administrator, access the Microsoft 365 Admin Center.

2. **Navigate to Deleted Sites:**

   o Under the **SharePoint Admin Center**, find the section labeled **Deleted Sites**.

3. **Select and Restore:**

   o Locate the deleted site in the list, select it, and click **Restore**.

Recovering Classic Sites:

For classic SharePoint sites, recovery options include using PowerShell commands or restoring backups if configured.

Using PowerShell to Restore a Site:

1. Open the SharePoint Management Shell.

2. Run the following command:

3. Restore-SPSite -Identity "https://yourdomain/sites/sitename" -DatabaseName "ContentDatabaseName"

4. Replace the placeholders with your actual site URL and database name.

Best Practices for Data Recovery

While SharePoint offers powerful recovery tools, it's always better to prevent data loss in the first place. Adopting the following best practices can reduce the need for recovery:

1. **Enable Versioning:**

   o Ensure document libraries and lists have versioning enabled. This allows users to restore previous versions of files without relying on the Recycle Bin.

2. **Backup Regularly:**

   o Configure regular backups for your SharePoint environment, either through third-party tools or native Microsoft solutions like Azure Backup.

3. **Educate Users:**

   o Provide training on SharePoint's recovery features to ensure team members know how to retrieve their files when needed.

4. **Set Appropriate Permissions:**

   o Restrict deletion rights to minimize the risk of accidental site or file deletions.

Handling Irreversible Deletions

In rare cases, items may be permanently deleted before they can be recovered. For example, if an item is purged from both stages of the Recycle Bin, it cannot be restored through SharePoint's native tools. In such situations:

- **Contact Microsoft Support:** Microsoft's support team can sometimes retrieve data that has been permanently deleted, depending on the time elapsed since deletion.

- **Utilize Backups:** Regularly maintained backups are invaluable for restoring irretrievable data.

Case Study: Avoiding Data Loss in a Large Organization

Imagine a scenario where an employee accidentally deletes an important project folder containing hundreds of documents. Thanks to SharePoint's versioning and Recycle Bin features, the IT administrator restores the entire folder within minutes. By configuring proper permissions and educating the team, the organization prevents future incidents and maintains business continuity.

By understanding and leveraging SharePoint's recovery tools, you can ensure that accidental deletions are never the end of the story. Effective data recovery not only saves time and resources but also builds confidence in SharePoint as a reliable collaboration platform.

8.3 Keeping Your Content Secure

8.3.1 Best Practices for Security

Security in SharePoint is a vital aspect of ensuring that your organization's sensitive data remains protected from unauthorized access or potential breaches. As SharePoint is used to store, share, and collaborate on critical documents and data, following robust security practices is non-negotiable. This section explores the best practices for maintaining a secure SharePoint environment, focusing on access controls, data encryption, compliance measures, and proactive threat management.

Understanding SharePoint's Security Model

SharePoint operates on a multi-layered security model designed to provide flexibility and control. The three key pillars of this model are:

- **Authentication**: Verifying the identity of users attempting to access the system.

- **Authorization**: Determining what actions authenticated users are permitted to perform.

- **Encryption**: Protecting data at rest and in transit to prevent unauthorized interception or tampering.

By understanding these layers, administrators can implement comprehensive strategies tailored to their organization's needs.

1. Implement Role-Based Access Control (RBAC)

Role-Based Access Control (RBAC) is a foundational practice for managing permissions in SharePoint. Rather than granting broad access to all users, permissions are assigned based on predefined roles, ensuring that individuals only have access to the data necessary for their job functions.

- **Define Clear Roles and Responsibilities**: Create roles such as "Reader," "Contributor," and "Owner," each with specific access rights.

- **Regularly Audit Roles**: Periodically review roles and permissions to ensure that they align with current team structures and responsibilities.

- **Use Groups for Permission Management**: Assign permissions to groups rather than individuals for easier management and scalability.

2. Leverage Multi-Factor Authentication (MFA)

Adding an extra layer of security, Multi-Factor Authentication (MFA) reduces the risk of unauthorized access even if a user's credentials are compromised. SharePoint integrates seamlessly with Microsoft's MFA solutions, allowing administrators to enforce its use across the organization.

- **Enable MFA for All Users**: Particularly for users with elevated privileges or those accessing SharePoint remotely.

- **Set Conditional Access Policies**: For example, require MFA only when users access SharePoint from untrusted networks or devices.

3. Encrypt Data in Transit and at Rest

Encryption is a critical component of SharePoint security, protecting data from being intercepted or accessed by unauthorized entities.

- **Data in Transit**: Ensure that all communications between users and SharePoint are encrypted using HTTPS protocols.

- **Data at Rest**: Use BitLocker encryption to safeguard stored data on SharePoint servers. SharePoint Online automatically encrypts data at rest using Microsoft-managed encryption keys.

For organizations requiring additional control, consider using **Customer Key** to manage your encryption keys for SharePoint Online.

4. Configure Secure Sharing Options

Sharing is one of SharePoint's most powerful features, but without proper controls, it can also be a security vulnerability.

- **Restrict Anonymous Sharing**: Disable sharing with anonymous links unless absolutely necessary.

- **Set Expiration Dates for Shared Links**: Prevent long-term access by setting time limits on external sharing links.

- **Monitor Shared Content**: Use SharePoint's built-in analytics to track who has accessed shared files and when.

5. Regularly Audit and Monitor Activity

Continuous monitoring and auditing are essential for detecting suspicious activity and ensuring compliance with security policies.

- **Enable Unified Audit Logs**: Track all user and admin activities across SharePoint to create an audit trail.

- **Use Alerts for Suspicious Behavior**: Set up alerts to notify administrators of unusual activities, such as mass file deletions or unauthorized access attempts.

- **Analyze Usage Patterns**: Leverage Microsoft Purview tools to gain insights into how data is being accessed and shared.

6. Maintain Data Compliance

SharePoint provides several features to help organizations meet industry-specific compliance requirements, such as GDPR, HIPAA, and ISO certifications.

- **Use Sensitivity Labels**: Classify and protect sensitive documents with labels that apply encryption and access restrictions automatically.

- **Implement Retention Policies**: Prevent accidental or malicious deletion of critical documents by configuring retention settings in SharePoint libraries.

- **Conduct Regular Compliance Audits**: Ensure that your SharePoint environment aligns with your organization's data protection policies.

7. Educate Users on Security Awareness

The human element is often the weakest link in any security strategy. A well-informed workforce is critical to preventing security breaches caused by phishing, social engineering, or accidental data exposure.

- **Conduct Regular Training**: Educate employees on best practices for secure file sharing, recognizing phishing attempts, and maintaining strong passwords.

- **Create Security Policies**: Clearly outline acceptable use policies for SharePoint and ensure employees are familiar with them.

- **Foster a Security-First Culture**: Encourage users to report suspicious activity and provide feedback on security measures.

8. Keep SharePoint Updated

Outdated software is a common entry point for cyberattacks. Microsoft regularly releases updates and patches for SharePoint to address vulnerabilities and enhance security.

- **Enable Automatic Updates**: For SharePoint Online, updates are applied automatically, ensuring that your environment is always running the latest version.

- **Apply On-Premises Patches Promptly**: For SharePoint Server, schedule regular maintenance windows to install updates and patches.

- **Test Updates in a Staging Environment**: Before applying updates to production, test them in a controlled environment to identify potential issues.

9. Back Up Your Data

Data loss can occur due to accidental deletions, hardware failures, or malicious attacks. Having a robust backup strategy ensures that you can recover critical information quickly.

- **Use Microsoft 365 Backup Solutions**: SharePoint Online offers built-in backup and recovery tools for deleted files and sites.

- **Implement Third-Party Backup Tools**: For more advanced backup requirements, consider third-party solutions that provide granular recovery options.

- **Test Your Backup Plan**: Regularly verify that backups are complete and that data can be restored successfully.

10. Plan for Disaster Recovery

Despite best efforts, breaches or data loss can still occur. A disaster recovery plan outlines the steps your organization will take to recover from these events.

- **Identify Critical Resources**: Determine which sites, libraries, and workflows are most critical to your operations.

- **Define Recovery Time Objectives (RTOs)**: Set realistic goals for how quickly systems should be restored.

- **Test Your Disaster Recovery Plan**: Conduct regular drills to ensure that your team is prepared to execute the plan effectively.

By implementing these best practices, you can significantly enhance the security of your SharePoint environment, protecting your organization's data and ensuring compliance with regulatory requirements. Security is not a one-time task but an ongoing process that requires vigilance, education, and adaptation to evolving threats.

8.3.2 Using Microsoft Defender

Microsoft Defender is a powerful tool within the Microsoft 365 ecosystem that enhances your SharePoint environment's security. Its integration ensures that your organization is protected against malware, phishing attempts, and other cyber threats. In this section, we'll explore how Microsoft Defender safeguards SharePoint content and how to configure it for maximum efficiency.

Understanding Microsoft Defender's Role in SharePoint Security

Microsoft Defender functions as a comprehensive security solution, providing advanced threat detection and response capabilities. For SharePoint, it offers:

- **Malware Detection:** Automatically scans files uploaded to SharePoint to ensure they are free from viruses and malicious code.

- **Real-Time Protection:** Identifies and blocks potential threats in real-time, preventing compromised files from being accessed or shared.

- **Advanced Threat Analytics:** Uses artificial intelligence (AI) to detect unusual activity patterns that may indicate a security breach.

- **Integration with Other Services:** Works seamlessly with Microsoft 365 apps such as Teams, OneDrive, and Exchange for unified threat protection.

Key Features of Microsoft Defender for SharePoint

1. **Automated Scanning:**

   Microsoft Defender scans files as they are uploaded to or downloaded from SharePoint libraries. This ensures that users cannot inadvertently introduce infected files into the environment.

2. **Threat Alerts:**

   Administrators receive notifications when suspicious activities are detected, such as attempts to access restricted files or upload malicious content.

3. **Behavioral Analysis:**

   Defender analyzes user behaviors, identifying anomalies such as repeated failed login attempts or unusual download patterns.

4. **Seamless Integration:**
   It integrates directly into SharePoint Online, eliminating the need for complex installations or configurations.

Setting Up Microsoft Defender for SharePoint

To use Microsoft Defender effectively, administrators need to configure it properly. Follow these steps to ensure optimal protection:

Step 1: Enable Microsoft Defender

Ensure that your Microsoft 365 subscription includes Microsoft Defender for Office 365. Navigate to the **Microsoft 365 Security & Compliance Center** to activate Defender for SharePoint.

Step 2: Configure Policies

Define security policies that align with your organization's requirements. This includes:

- **Malware Policies:** Specify how infected files should be handled (e.g., quarantine or automatic deletion).

- **Access Controls:** Limit access to sensitive content based on user roles and permissions.

Step 3: Set Up Alerts

Configure alert thresholds to notify administrators when suspicious activities occur. Use the **Threat Management Dashboard** to review and adjust alert settings.

Step 4: Monitor Activity

Regularly review activity logs in the Defender portal. This provides insights into potential vulnerabilities or areas requiring additional security measures.

Using Microsoft Defender to Mitigate Specific Risks

1. **Phishing Attacks:**

   Microsoft Defender helps detect and block phishing attempts by analyzing links and email attachments associated with SharePoint notifications.

2. **Ransomware Protection:**

Defender can identify and neutralize ransomware attempts by analyzing file behaviors, such as sudden bulk encryptions.

3. **Data Exfiltration:**

It monitors and flags unauthorized attempts to download or share sensitive data from SharePoint libraries.

Best Practices for Leveraging Microsoft Defender

1. **Regular Updates:**

Ensure that your Microsoft 365 environment, including Microsoft Defender, is always updated to the latest version. This keeps your system protected against emerging threats.

2. **Employee Training:**

Educate users about recognizing suspicious activities, such as unexpected file requests or unusual emails.

3. **Audit and Review:**

Periodically audit SharePoint sites and Microsoft Defender policies to identify gaps in security.

4. **Integrate with SIEM Tools:**

If your organization uses a Security Information and Event Management (SIEM) system, integrate Microsoft Defender logs for centralized monitoring.

5. **Enable Multi-Factor Authentication (MFA):**

Combine Defender with MFA to enhance account security.

Handling Security Incidents with Microsoft Defender

When a potential threat is detected, Microsoft Defender provides tools to respond effectively:

- **Quarantine Management:** View and manage quarantined files through the Security & Compliance Center.

- **Incident Investigation:** Use the incident tracker to trace the origin and scope of a detected threat.

- **Remediation Actions:** Apply recommended actions, such as blocking a user or resetting compromised credentials.

Case Study: Microsoft Defender in Action

Scenario: A user inadvertently uploads a malicious file to a SharePoint library.

1. **Detection:** Defender identifies the file as a threat during the upload process.

2. **Notification:** Administrators receive an alert with details about the file and the user.

3. **Action:** The file is automatically quarantined, and the user is temporarily restricted from uploading further content.

4. **Follow-Up:** IT reviews the incident, adjusts permissions, and educates the user on safe practices.

Conclusion

Microsoft Defender is a cornerstone of SharePoint security, offering robust tools to protect your data and users from evolving cyber threats. By configuring Defender thoughtfully and leveraging its features, you can create a secure, efficient SharePoint environment that supports your organization's collaboration needs without compromising safety.

Conclusion

9.1 Summary of Key Features

SharePoint has become an essential tool for organizations of all sizes, offering a robust platform for collaboration, document management, and workflow automation. This section provides a comprehensive summary of its key features, highlighting how SharePoint empowers users and organizations to achieve their goals efficiently.

1. Centralized Document Management

One of SharePoint's most significant advantages is its ability to serve as a centralized hub for document storage and management. This feature eliminates the need for scattered files across multiple systems, ensuring that all documents are accessible in one location. Key functionalities include:

- **Version Control**: SharePoint tracks changes to documents, enabling users to view, restore, or compare previous versions easily.

- **Metadata and Tags**: Adding metadata helps organize files and makes them searchable, improving efficiency in retrieving documents.

- **Co-Authoring**: Multiple users can work on a document simultaneously, with changes synchronized in real-time.

2. Customizable Sites

SharePoint provides the flexibility to create and customize sites tailored to specific needs. Whether it's a team site for internal collaboration or a communication site to share updates with a broader audience, SharePoint caters to diverse requirements. Key site customization features include:

- **Templates**: Pre-designed templates for team sites, communication sites, and hub sites simplify the setup process.

- **Web Parts**: These building blocks allow users to add functionality to pages, such as calendars, task lists, and newsfeeds.

- **Themes and Branding**: Users can personalize site themes to align with their organization's branding.

3. Enhanced Collaboration Tools

SharePoint fosters seamless collaboration through a suite of integrated tools:

- **Shared Workspaces**: Team members can share files, track tasks, and manage projects within a shared environment.

- **Discussion Boards**: These allow teams to have threaded discussions, ensuring clarity and context in communication.

- **Integration with Microsoft Teams**: SharePoint integrates deeply with Teams, enabling users to share files and collaborate directly from the Teams interface.

4. Powerful Search Capabilities

The robust search functionality in SharePoint allows users to quickly locate content, even in large repositories. Features include:

- **Search Refiners**: Filters such as file type, author, and date help narrow down results.

- **AI-Powered Search**: SharePoint leverages artificial intelligence to deliver relevant results based on user behavior and organizational context.

- **Search Across Content Types**: Users can search for documents, lists, sites, and even conversations within a single interface.

5. Integration with Microsoft 365

SharePoint seamlessly integrates with the Microsoft 365 ecosystem, enhancing productivity and collaboration. Key integrations include:

- **Outlook**: Sync calendars and emails with SharePoint to streamline scheduling and communication.

- **Power Automate**: Automate workflows and processes directly from SharePoint.

- **Power BI**: Visualize data with interactive dashboards embedded in SharePoint pages.

6. Scalability and Flexibility

SharePoint scales to meet the needs of organizations, whether they are small startups or large enterprises. Its cloud-based infrastructure in SharePoint Online ensures that it remains flexible and adaptive to evolving demands. Highlights include:

- **Custom Development**: Advanced users can build custom apps and solutions using PowerApps or SharePoint Framework (SPFx).

- **Third-Party Integrations**: SharePoint supports integration with numerous third-party applications, expanding its capabilities.

- **Mobile Accessibility**: The SharePoint mobile app ensures that users can access content and collaborate on the go.

7. Robust Security and Compliance

Security is a cornerstone of SharePoint's design, making it a trusted platform for sensitive organizational data. Its security features include:

- **Granular Permissions**: Control access at the site, document library, folder, or file level.

- **Data Encryption**: Ensure that data is protected both in transit and at rest.

- **Compliance Tools**: Built-in compliance features, such as audit logs and data retention policies, support regulatory requirements.

8. Automated Workflows and Process Management

SharePoint empowers users to streamline repetitive tasks through automation. Features include:

- **Workflows**: Automate approvals, notifications, and document routing.

- **Power Automate Integration**: Build sophisticated workflows to connect SharePoint with other Microsoft 365 apps and external systems.

- **Task Management**: SharePoint integrates with Microsoft Planner to assign and track tasks effectively.

9. Dynamic List and Library Features

SharePoint's lists and libraries are powerful tools for managing structured data and documents. Key features include:

- **Customizable Columns**: Create columns to store specific types of data.

- **Views**: Customize how data is displayed with personal or shared views.

- **Data Validation**: Enforce rules to ensure data accuracy and consistency.

10. Insights and Analytics

SharePoint provides insights to help organizations make data-driven decisions.

- **Site Analytics**: Monitor user activity and site usage trends.

- **Search Insights**: Analyze search patterns to identify gaps in content.

- **Power BI Dashboards**: Generate comprehensive reports directly from SharePoint data.

11. Mobile and Remote Accessibility

With remote work becoming the norm, SharePoint ensures that users can remain productive from anywhere.

- **Responsive Design**: SharePoint sites are optimized for various screen sizes.

- **Offline Access**: Sync files for offline use and upload changes once reconnected.

- **Cross-Platform Compatibility**: Access SharePoint on Windows, macOS, iOS, and Android devices.

12. Future-Ready Platform

SharePoint evolves continuously, incorporating emerging technologies to remain relevant. Upcoming trends include:

- **AI and Machine Learning**: Improved content recommendations and task automation.

- **Deeper Integrations**: Enhanced compatibility with Microsoft's expanding suite of tools.

- **Hybrid Environments**: Continued support for on-premises and cloud deployments.

Closing Thoughts

The features summarized above showcase SharePoint's versatility as a comprehensive platform for modern workplaces. From document management to advanced analytics, SharePoint empowers users to work smarter, collaborate more effectively, and drive organizational success. Understanding and leveraging these features will help you maximize the value SharePoint brings to your team and organization.

9.2 Future Trends in SharePoint

As one of the most widely used platforms for collaboration and content management, SharePoint continues to evolve rapidly to meet the needs of modern businesses. The future of SharePoint is intertwined with broader technological trends, such as cloud computing, artificial intelligence (AI), and machine learning. In this section, we will explore the key trends shaping the future of SharePoint and how these advancements will impact users, organizations, and IT professionals.

1. The Rise of Cloud-First Strategy

One of the biggest trends influencing SharePoint's future is the increasing adoption of a cloud-first strategy. While SharePoint has traditionally been available as both an on-premises solution and a cloud-based service, Microsoft has made it clear that the future of SharePoint lies in the cloud. With the launch of SharePoint Online, part of the Office 365 suite, Microsoft has provided businesses with a more flexible and scalable solution that integrates seamlessly with other cloud services.

Cloud-based SharePoint environments offer significant advantages over traditional on-premises deployments. They provide better scalability, cost-effectiveness, and the ability to access files and documents from any device, anywhere in the world. As more companies transition to the cloud, the demand for hybrid solutions that combine on-premises and cloud deployments is also increasing. SharePoint's continued integration with the broader Microsoft 365 ecosystem will make it a central hub for collaboration and productivity tools in the cloud.

2. Enhanced Artificial Intelligence and Automation

Artificial intelligence (AI) and automation are reshaping many industries, and SharePoint is no exception. Microsoft is increasingly embedding AI capabilities within SharePoint to improve user experiences and streamline workflows. These enhancements will help users work smarter and faster while reducing the time spent on manual tasks.

One key example of AI integration in SharePoint is **Microsoft Search**, powered by AI, which allows users to search across multiple Microsoft 365 apps, including SharePoint, to find relevant content more efficiently. The AI-backed search functionality is designed to deliver personalized results based on user behavior, work patterns, and preferences.

Additionally, **Power Automate** (formerly Microsoft Flow) integrates with SharePoint to automate workflows, saving time and reducing the likelihood of errors. For instance, workflows can be set up to automatically trigger document approvals, notify users of important changes, or update lists based on certain conditions. As AI continues to evolve, SharePoint will likely see even more intelligent automation features, such as automated content categorization, document tagging, and advanced content insights.

3. Integration with Microsoft Teams and Other Tools

The integration between SharePoint and Microsoft Teams is one of the most significant developments in recent years. With the increasing shift toward remote work and digital collaboration, Teams has become the go-to platform for team communication. SharePoint serves as the backend for document storage and collaboration within Teams, and this integration will continue to deepen in the future.

Expect to see **more seamless collaboration** between SharePoint and Microsoft Teams, with enhanced capabilities for managing files, documents, and team communication directly from within Teams. The deepening integration will allow users to interact with SharePoint documents, lists, and libraries without having to switch between multiple apps.

In addition, SharePoint will continue to integrate with other Microsoft 365 tools such as OneDrive, Planner, and Outlook. This interconnected ecosystem of tools will enable teams to collaborate and share information more efficiently, reducing the need for users to constantly switch between different platforms and services.

4. Modern Experience and User Interface (UI) Enhancements

SharePoint has come a long way from its early versions, and its user interface (UI) continues to evolve to meet modern expectations. The **SharePoint modern experience**, introduced in recent years, represents a major shift toward a more intuitive and user-friendly interface. This modern design focuses on delivering a faster, cleaner, and more responsive experience for users, especially those who may not have a deep technical background.

In the future, we can expect further refinements to the SharePoint UI, with an emphasis on **mobile responsiveness**, **personalization**, and **enhanced accessibility**. As more users access SharePoint from mobile devices and tablets, ensuring that the platform provides a seamless experience across all devices will be a priority for Microsoft.

SharePoint pages and sites will become even more customizable and visually appealing, allowing users to design interactive and engaging content without requiring extensive coding knowledge. This focus on personalization will enable businesses to tailor SharePoint environments to meet specific team or organizational needs, improving user engagement and satisfaction.

5. Improved Collaboration with External Partners

As businesses increasingly work with external partners, contractors, and clients, there is a growing demand for secure and seamless collaboration beyond the corporate firewall. SharePoint will continue to improve its **external sharing capabilities**, making it easier for organizations to collaborate with third parties while maintaining strict security controls.

The **sharing features** in SharePoint allow users to invite external collaborators to view or edit documents, participate in discussions, or contribute to project sites. Microsoft has been steadily enhancing these features, offering more granular control over sharing permissions and providing better ways to track and manage external access. In the future, we can expect even more sophisticated options for securely sharing content with external partners, including improved **multi-factor authentication (MFA)** and **identity verification**.

6. Data Governance and Compliance

As data privacy regulations such as the General Data Protection Regulation (GDPR) and the California Consumer Privacy Act (CCPA) become increasingly important, organizations need robust tools for **data governance** and **compliance**. SharePoint will continue to evolve to meet these needs, providing businesses with the tools they need to comply with regulatory requirements.

Compliance Center in Microsoft 365, which includes SharePoint, already helps businesses manage compliance risks, but future updates will likely make it even easier to monitor and control access to sensitive data. Features such as **data loss prevention (DLP)**, **retention policies**, and **auditing tools** will continue to be refined to provide greater protection for users and organizations.

Additionally, SharePoint will likely continue to embrace **artificial intelligence** to help automate compliance monitoring, flagging potential issues before they become problems.

AI could be used to monitor document usage patterns and automatically apply compliance rules based on document content and context.

7. Custom Development and Low-Code Solutions

Another area where SharePoint is expected to grow is in its **customization and development capabilities**. SharePoint already supports powerful customization tools, such as SharePoint Framework (SPFx) for building custom web parts and applications. However, the future of SharePoint will see a greater focus on **low-code and no-code solutions**, allowing users with little or no programming experience to create custom solutions that fit their unique needs.

The **Power Platform**, which includes **Power Apps**, **Power Automate**, and **Power BI**, will continue to integrate with SharePoint to enable businesses to build custom applications and workflows. These low-code tools will empower non-developers to design solutions that automate tasks, collect and analyze data, and create custom user interfaces.

SharePoint's integration with the Power Platform will make it easier for businesses to create tailored workflows and applications without relying on IT teams for custom development. As the demand for more personalized solutions grows, SharePoint will likely become even more flexible and accessible for business users.

8. Focus on Sustainability and Green IT

As sustainability becomes a key concern for businesses worldwide, SharePoint will play a role in helping organizations reduce their carbon footprint. **Green IT** initiatives, which focus on reducing the environmental impact of technology, are gaining traction. Microsoft's commitment to becoming **carbon-neutral** by 2030 will likely drive further innovations in SharePoint to support sustainability goals.

SharePoint's cloud infrastructure, hosted on Microsoft's data centers, already has a low carbon footprint, and future updates may further improve energy efficiency and sustainability. Microsoft's efforts to **optimize server utilization**, reduce waste, and promote energy-efficient technologies will likely influence SharePoint's development and help businesses achieve their sustainability objectives.

Conclusion

The future of SharePoint is bright, with continuous improvements being made in areas such as cloud computing, artificial intelligence, automation, and customization. As businesses face increasing demands for better collaboration, enhanced security, and improved productivity, SharePoint will continue to evolve to meet these challenges.

With its integration into the broader Microsoft 365 ecosystem, SharePoint will remain a central hub for collaboration, document management, and business process automation. By embracing these trends, businesses can ensure that their SharePoint environment is not only up-to-date but also equipped to handle the demands of the future.

9.3 Final Tips for Success

As you conclude your journey into the world of SharePoint, it's essential to carry forward a few key principles and strategies to ensure long-term success. SharePoint is a powerful tool, but its effectiveness depends on how you use it to meet your organization's unique needs. In this section, we will discuss practical tips to help you maximize your experience with SharePoint, enhance team collaboration, and maintain a productive and efficient workflow.

Embrace Continuous Learning

SharePoint is a dynamic platform, with frequent updates and new features being introduced by Microsoft. Staying informed about these changes is vital to ensure that you're leveraging the latest tools and functionalities. Here's how to embrace a mindset of continuous learning:

- **Follow Official Channels**: Subscribe to Microsoft's blogs, forums, and newsletters related to SharePoint to keep up with updates and best practices.

- **Participate in Webinars and Training Sessions**: Many organizations, including Microsoft, offer free or paid training sessions. These sessions provide insights into advanced features or upcoming developments.

- **Engage in the SharePoint Community**: Join online forums or local user groups where SharePoint professionals share knowledge, troubleshoot issues, and exchange tips.

Prioritize User Training and Support

Your organization's success with SharePoint depends heavily on how well users understand and adopt the platform. Even the best-configured SharePoint environment can falter without proper user engagement.

- **Develop Comprehensive Training Programs**: Ensure all users, from beginners to advanced, have access to tailored training. Offer interactive tutorials, live sessions, and written guides.

- **Create an Internal Support System**: Establish a team or designate power users who can assist others with SharePoint issues. A responsive support system can greatly enhance user satisfaction.

- **Encourage Feedback**: Regularly solicit user input to identify pain points and areas for improvement. This feedback can guide future training and customization efforts.

Maintain a Well-Structured Environment

One of SharePoint's key strengths is its ability to organize information. However, without proper management, your SharePoint environment can become cluttered and difficult to navigate.

- **Implement a Governance Plan**: A governance plan outlines rules for managing sites, content, and user permissions. It helps maintain consistency and ensures compliance with organizational policies.

- **Organize Content Effectively**: Use logical folder structures, metadata, and tagging to make files and information easy to find. Encourage users to follow these structures.

- **Regularly Archive and Delete Unused Content**: Periodically review your SharePoint sites and libraries to identify outdated or unnecessary content. Archiving or deleting this content can free up space and improve performance.

Leverage Automation

Automation can save time and reduce human error, making your SharePoint workflows more efficient.

- **Explore Power Automate**: Microsoft Power Automate allows you to create workflows that automate repetitive tasks. For instance, you can set up alerts for document approvals or automate file organization.

- **Utilize Built-in SharePoint Features**: SharePoint has several native automation tools, such as workflows and alerts. Familiarize yourself with these features to streamline daily operations.

- **Monitor and Optimize Workflows**: Regularly review automated processes to ensure they remain relevant and effective as your organization's needs evolve.

Focus on Security

Security should always be a top priority when managing your SharePoint environment. With sensitive organizational data stored on the platform, ensuring its protection is non-negotiable.

- **Implement Role-Based Access Controls (RBAC)**: Assign user roles based on their responsibilities. For example, only allow certain users to edit sensitive documents while others have view-only access.

- **Enable Multi-Factor Authentication (MFA)**: Adding an extra layer of security ensures that only authorized users can access your SharePoint sites.

- **Regularly Audit Permissions**: Periodically review user permissions to ensure that only authorized individuals have access to specific data or features.

Encourage Collaboration and Engagement

SharePoint is most effective when it fosters collaboration and teamwork. Here's how to make the platform a cornerstone of your team's workflow:

- **Promote Transparency**: Use SharePoint's shared workspaces and document libraries to create a culture of openness. This allows everyone to stay updated and contribute effectively.

- **Celebrate Success Stories**: Highlight successful projects or initiatives completed using SharePoint. Sharing these stories can inspire others to adopt the platform more enthusiastically.

- **Integrate with Other Tools**: Leverage integrations with Microsoft Teams, Outlook, and Power BI to create a seamless digital workspace.

Monitor Performance and Plan for Growth

Your SharePoint needs will evolve as your organization grows. Keeping a close eye on performance and planning for scalability will help you stay ahead.

- **Use SharePoint Analytics**: Leverage built-in analytics tools to monitor site usage, identify popular features, and track areas for improvement.

- **Prepare for Storage Needs**: Monitor your storage usage and plan for upgrades if needed. This ensures that your SharePoint environment continues to perform well even as content increases.

- **Plan for Migration and Updates**: If your organization plans to switch to a newer SharePoint version or integrate with other tools, start planning early to minimize disruptions.

Foster a Growth Mindset

Finally, the most important tip for success with SharePoint is to cultivate a growth mindset. SharePoint is not a static tool; it's a platform that evolves alongside your organization. By staying adaptable, embracing change, and fostering innovation, you can unlock SharePoint's full potential.

Encourage your team to experiment with new features, share ideas for improvement, and explore creative solutions. With the right mindset and a strategic approach, SharePoint can become a cornerstone of your organization's digital transformation journey.

Appendices

A. SharePoint Keyboard Shortcuts

Mastering keyboard shortcuts can significantly enhance your efficiency when working with SharePoint. These shortcuts allow you to quickly navigate, perform tasks, and manage content without relying solely on your mouse. This section outlines essential SharePoint keyboard shortcuts categorized by their usage, providing you with a practical reference to improve your workflow.

A.1 Navigation Shortcuts

Efficient navigation is vital when managing SharePoint sites, libraries, and pages. These shortcuts will help you move around quickly:

- **Tab**: Move focus to the next element on a page.
- **Shift + Tab**: Move focus to the previous element on a page.
- **Enter**: Activate the selected link or button.
- **Alt + Q**: Open the Search box in SharePoint Online.
- **Alt + F**: Open the File menu for site options (browser-dependent).

Practical Tips for Navigation:

- Combine **Tab** and **Enter** to navigate between sections and select actions.
- Use **Shift + Tab** to revisit missed elements without restarting navigation from the top.

A.2 Document and Library Management Shortcuts

SharePoint's document libraries are central to its functionality. Use these shortcuts to manage files and folders effectively:

- **Ctrl + N**: Create a new document or folder in the library.

- **Ctrl + S**: Save changes to a document (when editing online).

- **Ctrl + P**: Print the current document.

- **Alt + N**: Open the "New" menu to add a file, folder, or link.

- **Alt + E**: Edit the selected document or item.

- **Alt + U**: Upload files to the current library.

- **Delete**: Delete the selected document or item.

Example Scenario:

When working on a project, you can use **Ctrl + N** to quickly create folders for organizing files and **Ctrl + S** to save progress while editing documents.

A.3 Editing and Formatting Shortcuts

SharePoint pages and lists often require formatting and content editing. Here are shortcuts to speed up the process:

- **Ctrl + B**: Bold selected text.

- **Ctrl + I**: Italicize selected text.

- **Ctrl + U**: Underline selected text.

- **Ctrl + X**: Cut selected content.

- **Ctrl + C**: Copy selected content.

- **Ctrl + V**: Paste copied content.

- **Ctrl + Z**: Undo the last action.

- **Ctrl + Y**: Redo the last undone action.

Editing Tip:

When creating SharePoint pages, use **Ctrl + B**, **Ctrl + I**, and **Ctrl + U** to emphasize key points in your content.

A.4 Data Entry in Lists

When entering or editing data in SharePoint lists, these shortcuts are indispensable:

- **Tab**: Move to the next cell in a list or table.

- **Shift + Tab**: Move to the previous cell.

- **Enter**: Save the data in the current cell and move to the next row.

- **Esc**: Cancel data entry in the current cell.

- **Ctrl + Space**: Select the entire row.

- **Shift + Space**: Select the entire column.

Data Entry Scenario:

If you're updating inventory data in a SharePoint list, use **Tab** to move between fields and **Enter** to quickly save each entry.

A.5 Accessibility Shortcuts

SharePoint provides robust support for accessibility. These shortcuts are tailored for screen reader users and keyboard-only navigation:

- **Alt + Shift + 1**: Navigate to the main content area.

- **Alt + Shift + 2**: Navigate to the quick launch bar.

- **Alt + Shift + 3**: Navigate to the top navigation bar.

- **Alt + Shift + 0**: Access the Accessibility Help menu.

Accessibility Highlight:

These shortcuts ensure that all users, regardless of ability, can interact effectively with SharePoint.

A.6 Calendar and Task Management Shortcuts

Managing events and tasks in SharePoint is easier with these shortcuts:

- **Ctrl + N**: Create a new event or task.

- **Ctrl + E**: Edit the selected event or task.

- **Ctrl + D**: Delete the selected event or task.

- **Ctrl + T**: Toggle between task views (list, calendar, or Gantt chart).

Real-Life Usage:

Plan your team's weekly meetings by creating events using **Ctrl + N** and updating details with **Ctrl + E**.

A.7 Search and Filter Shortcuts

Efficiently finding and filtering content is essential in SharePoint. Use these shortcuts to enhance your search capabilities:

- **Ctrl + F**: Open the browser's Find feature to locate text on a page.

- **Alt + S**: Open the Search bar in SharePoint.

- **Ctrl + Shift + F**: Advanced filtering options in libraries or lists.

- **Alt + X**: Clear applied filters.

Advanced Search Example:

When locating a specific policy document, use **Alt + S** to search the library and refine results with **Ctrl + Shift + F**.

A.8 Customizing Shortcuts

If you use specific features frequently, you can customize shortcuts using SharePoint's integration with Microsoft Power Automate or third-party tools.

- Create custom workflows for repetitive tasks.

- Assign macros to keys for direct actions (e.g., approval workflows).

Customization Tip:

Explore Power Automate to design shortcuts that align with your daily tasks.

A.9 Summary Table of Shortcuts

Below is a quick reference table summarizing essential SharePoint shortcuts:

Action	Shortcut	Category
Move to Next Element	Tab	Navigation
Save Document	Ctrl + S	Document Management
Bold Text	Ctrl + B	Editing
Create New Task	Ctrl + N	Task Management
Search SharePoint	Alt + S	Search and Filter

This table can be printed and kept as a handy guide while working in SharePoint.

By incorporating these shortcuts into your workflow, you'll save time, reduce effort, and gain confidence in navigating and managing SharePoint environments. Practice these shortcuts regularly, and you'll soon master SharePoint's full potential!

B. Glossary of Terms

The following glossary provides definitions for key terms commonly used in SharePoint. Understanding these terms will help you navigate the platform more effectively and utilize its features to their full potential.

A

Access Permissions: The rules and settings that determine what users can view, edit, or delete in a SharePoint environment.

Active Directory: A directory service used by Microsoft to manage network resources and user permissions, often integrated with SharePoint.

Alerts: Notifications sent to users when changes occur in lists, libraries, or other SharePoint features they are following.

App Launcher: A menu in the Office 365 suite that provides quick access to SharePoint and other applications.

B

Breadcrumb Navigation: A visual aid that helps users understand their location within a site and navigate back to previous pages or sections.

Business Connectivity Services (BCS): A SharePoint service that allows integration of external data from systems like SQL databases or web services.

C

Content Type: A reusable collection of settings for a specific type of content, such as documents, items, or pages, enabling consistent metadata and workflows.

Co-Authoring: A feature that allows multiple users to edit a document simultaneously in SharePoint.

Custom List: A list created by users to track specific data, such as tasks, inventory, or event registrations, tailored to their needs.

D

Document Library: A specialized library in SharePoint for storing, organizing, and managing files such as Word documents, PDFs, or Excel spreadsheets.

Drag-and-Drop Upload: A feature that allows users to upload files by dragging them into a SharePoint library.

Discussion Board: A feature in SharePoint for creating and participating in threaded discussions, often used for team collaboration.

E

Excel Services: A SharePoint feature that allows users to view and interact with Excel workbooks directly in a browser.

External Sharing: A SharePoint feature that enables users to share content with individuals outside their organization, such as clients or partners.

F

Forms: Interactive pages created in SharePoint or integrated tools like PowerApps, used for gathering data from users.

Folder: A container within a library or list used to organize files or items into groups.

H

Hub Site: A SharePoint site that connects and organizes related sites, providing a unified navigation structure and shared features.

I

Intranet: An internal network where SharePoint often serves as a platform for company-wide communication and collaboration.

Item: A single entry in a SharePoint list, such as a task, event, or contact.

K

Key Performance Indicators (KPIs): Metrics displayed in SharePoint to track progress against organizational goals.

L

Lists: A feature in SharePoint for organizing and managing structured data, such as tasks, contacts, or events.
Library: A repository in SharePoint used for storing and managing files or content.

M

Metadata: Information about content in SharePoint, such as tags, categories, or custom properties, used for organization and search.
Modern Pages: The newer, more dynamic type of page in SharePoint, designed for improved usability and mobile responsiveness.

N

Navigation: The menus and links in SharePoint that help users move between pages, sites, and features.
Newsfeed: A SharePoint feature that aggregates updates and discussions for a site or organization.

P

Permissions: The rights assigned to users or groups in SharePoint to access or manage content and settings.
Power Automate: A tool integrated with SharePoint for automating workflows and repetitive tasks.

S

Search: A powerful tool in SharePoint that helps users locate files, items, and other content across sites.
SharePoint Online: The cloud-based version of SharePoint, accessible through Microsoft 365.
Site: A workspace within SharePoint, designed for collaboration, document sharing, or information dissemination.
Site Collection: A grouping of related SharePoint sites under a single top-level site.

T

Team Site: A type of SharePoint site designed for team collaboration, including shared documents, calendars, and tasks.
Template: A predefined layout or configuration for creating new SharePoint sites, lists, or libraries.

U

User Group: A collection of users with shared permissions in SharePoint, often managed for easier access control.

V

Version History: A SharePoint feature that tracks changes to files and items, allowing users to view or restore previous versions.
Views: Customizable ways to display data in lists or libraries, such as sorting, filtering, or grouping items.

W

Web Part: A customizable widget or module that can be added to a SharePoint page to display specific content or functionality.

Workflow: An automated sequence of actions in SharePoint used for tasks like approvals or notifications.

Y

Yammer: A Microsoft tool integrated with SharePoint for enterprise social networking and communication.

This glossary covers the foundational terms you'll encounter while working with SharePoint. By familiarizing yourself with these definitions, you'll have a stronger grasp of the platform and its capabilities. If you encounter additional terms during your journey with SharePoint, use this glossary as a starting point for understanding and exploration.

Acknowledgment

*Thank you for choosing **SharePoint Solutions: A Practical User Guide**. Your decision to invest in this book means a great deal to me, and I truly appreciate the trust you've placed in this guide to help you navigate and master SharePoint.*

Writing this book has been a journey of exploring ways to simplify complex concepts and present them in a way that empowers users like you. I hope the content meets your expectations and provides practical insights that make your SharePoint experience more productive and enjoyable.

Your support not only motivates me but also contributes to the broader mission of making technology accessible and understandable for everyone. Whether you're a professional, a student, or someone curious about SharePoint, I am grateful to have played a role in your learning journey.

If you found this book helpful, I would be thrilled if you could share your thoughts, leave a review, or recommend it to others who might benefit from it. Your feedback is invaluable and inspires future works aimed at enhancing user experiences.

Thank you once again for your support, and I wish you success in all your endeavors with SharePoint. May it be a tool that helps you achieve great things!

Warm regards,

www.ingramcontent.com/pod-product-compliance
Lightning Source LLC
LaVergne TN
LVHW062310060326
832902LV00013B/2134